AF600402

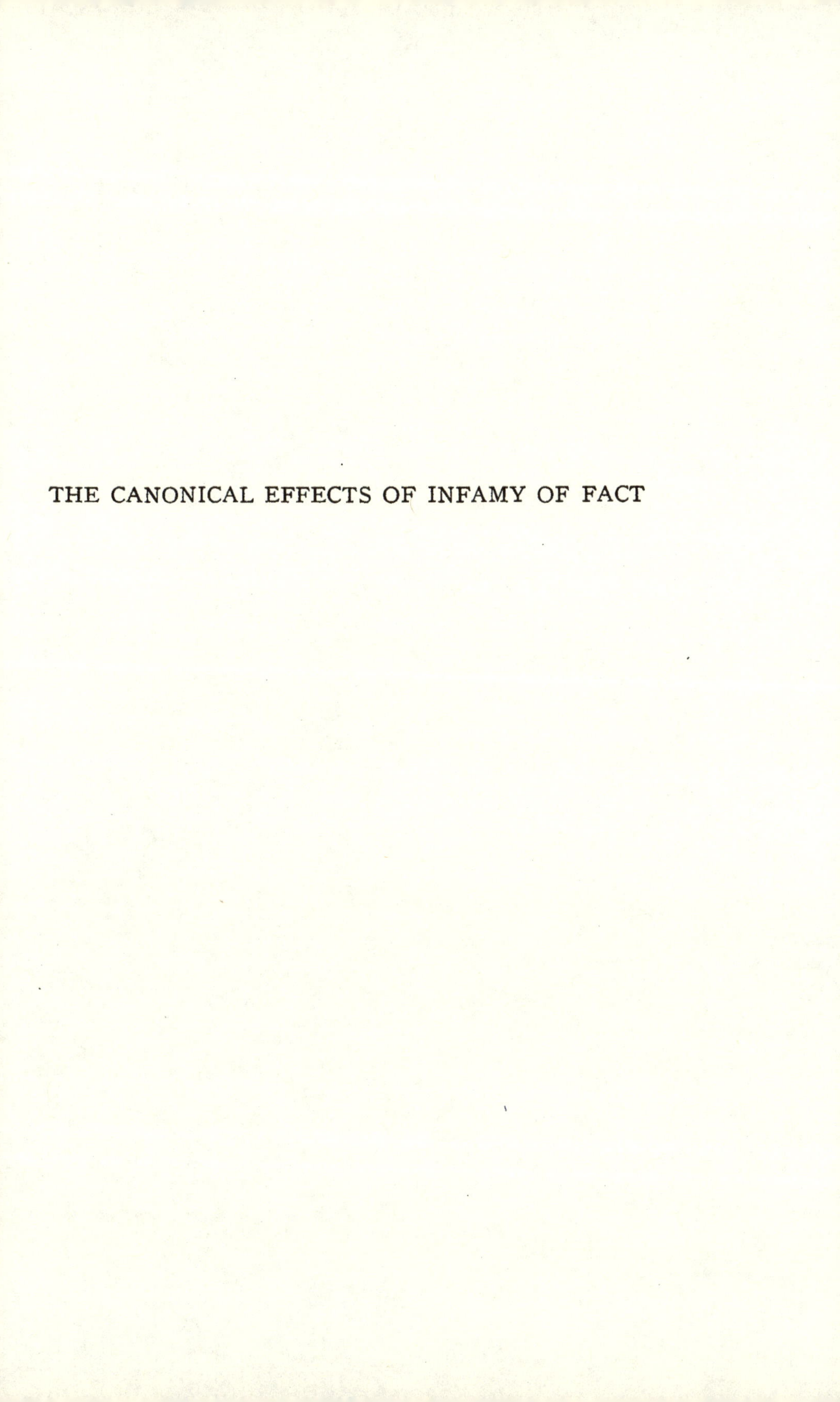

THE CANONICAL EFFECTS OF INFAMY OF FACT

THE CATHOLIC UNIVERSITY OF AMERICA
CANON LAW STUDIES
No. 353

The Canonical Effects of Infamy of Fact

A HISTORICAL SYNOPSIS AND A COMMENTARY

A DISSERTATION
SUBMITTED TO THE FACULTY OF THE SCHOOL OF CANON LAW OF THE CATHOLIC UNIVERSITY OF AMERICA IN PARTIAL FULFILLMENT OF THE REQUIREMENTS FOR THE DEGREE OF DOCTOR OF CANON LAW

BY
REV. FRANK J. RODIMER, A.B., S.T.L., J.C.L.
PRIEST OF THE DIOCESE OF PATERSON

THE CATHOLIC UNIVERSITY OF AMERICA PRESS
WASHINGTON, D. C.
1954

NIHIL OBSTAT:

THOMAS O. MARTIN, PH.D, S.T.D., J.C.D.
Censor Deputatus

Washingtonii, D.C., die 6 aprilis, 1954

IMPRIMATUR:

✠ JACOBUS A. MCNULTY, D.D.
Episcopus Patersonensis

Patersonii, die 9 aprilis, 1954

Printed by Theo. Gaus' Sons, Inc., Brooklyn 1, N. Y., U. S. A.

TABLE OF CONTENTS

TABLE OF CONTENTS (Continued)

PART II

CANONICAL COMMENTARY

TABLE OF CONTENTS (Continued)

FOREWORD

Man has always found it essential to his happiness that he be respected by his fellow man. He cannot be denied the respect of society for a long time, and live a normal, happy and successful life. Such a loss of the esteem of one's fellows is, then, a hardship, a punishment. This loss of one's good reputation has been called *"infamia,"* and is of two types. *Infamia iuris* is a penalty, a vindicative penalty, inflicted by law on those who are guilty of certain grave crimes specified in the law. *Infamia facti* is, in a certain sense, a "penalty," one of the natural order, whereby one loses his good name because he is guilty of some crime or because he leads a sinful life.

Infamia facti, however, is not a penalty in the strict sense of the word. It is a natural reaction of good and prudent men to the misdeeds of their fellow men. It is, in a way, the judgment of God Himself made known through the judgment of men. *"Vox populi, vox Dei,"* said Alcuin, the eighth century theologian, in one of his many letters to Charlemagne. Infamy of fact is only in the broadest sense, then, a punishment, one whereby a man loses his good reputation because of his sins.

The Church's concept of *infamia* in general is adopted from *infamia* as it appeared in the Roman Law. It was, in the Roman legal system, a penalty whereby, as far as the legal authorities were concerned, a culprit was undeserving of any respect. The Church adopted this punishment of infamy into its own legislation and always applied it to the most despicable of crimes.

There is discernible in Roman Law and in Canon Law, however, a distinction between the penal *infamia* and that factual *infamia* which, though it prescinds from any penalty in the strict sense of the word, is an actual loss of reputation. The medieval canonists gave the name *"infamia facti"* to this actual loss of one's good name to distinguish it from the penalty they labeled *"infamia iuris."* Although infamy of fact was adverted to in the provisions of the earlier laws, it remained for the Code of Canon Law to provide the first official and legal descriptive definition of *infamia facti*: "Infamy of fact is contracted when a person, either because of a crime he has committed or because of corrupt morals, has lost his good repute among upright and earnest members of the faithful, the determination of which facts is left to the judgment of the Ordinary."[1] It is this infamy of fact which is dealt with in this work, and, more specifically, the effects of such a loss of reputation in so far as these effects are established in the Code.

It is hoped that this work will, on the one hand, present faithfully the Church's solicitude for one of man's most priceless possessions, his reputation, and, on the other, will explain properly the Church's precautions in preserving free from disgrace its noble and sacred functions and offices by delivering them from the hands of those who have lost their good standing in society.

I am especially grateful to the Most Reverend Thomas A. Boland, Archbishop of Newark, who as Bishop of Paterson first gave me the opportunity to pursue graduate studies in Canon Law at The Catholic University of America; to the Most Reverend James A. McNulty, Bishop of Paterson, who made it possible for me to complete these studies; to all members of the Faculty of the School of Canon Law for their assistance with this dissertation and with the study of Canon Law in general; and to all who have helped in any way in the preparation of this dissertation.

---

[1] Canon 2293, §3.

PART I

HISTORICAL SYNOPSIS

CHAPTER I

The Notion of Infamy of Fact Before the Code

Atricle I. *Infamia Facti* in the Roman Law

The legislation of the Code of Canon Law in regard to infamy has as its basis the system of *infamia* in the Roman law.[1]

Though it is not known with certainty how this legislation concerning *infamia* originated in Roman law, the noteworthy similarity between the censorian *notatio* and infamy leads authors to believe that it began with the censorship in 443 B.C.[2]

As a census-taker, the censor applied a mark (*nota*) alongside the names of those whom he knew to be guilty of some grave offense, and thus branded them as people who should be punished.[3]

Towards the close of the Republic, the censor ceased to exercise the old functions, and the vacancy thus created was supplied by the *Praetor Urbanus,* which office had been established in 367 B.C. The praetor at the beginning of his term of office issued an edict. In this edict he listed those to whom as persons of tarnished reputation he would refuse the full *ius postulandi* (i.e., the right to make application to the court otherwise than on behalf of themselves or certain close relatives).[4] He also named in the edict those to whom as persons of tarnished reputation he would not grant the

---

[1] Cocchi, *Commentarium in Codicem Iuris Canonici* (8 vols., Vol. VIII, 4. ed., Taurinorum Augustae: Marietti, 1938), VIII, 192 (hereafter cited as *Commentarium*); Chelodi-Ciprotti, *Ius Canonicum de Delictis et Poenis* (3. ed., Trento: Libraria Moderna Editrice, 1943), n. 50, p. 66 (hereafter cited as *De Delictis*).

[2] Buckland, *Manual of Roman Private Law* (London: Cambridge University Press, 1925), p. 53 (hereafter cited as Buckland); Leage, *Roman Private Law* (2. ed. by C. H. Ziegler, London: MacMillan and Co., 1930; reprinted, 1948), pp. 29-30 (hereafter cited as Leage).

[3] Lee, *The Elements of Roman Law* (London: Sweet and Maxwell Ltd., 1944), p. 208 (hereafter cited as Lee).

[4] Sohm, *The Institutes* (3. ed., Oxford: At the Clarendon Press, 1926), p. 183 (hereafter cited as Sohm).

right of acting as the agent of another in an action (*alieno nomine agere*) or of being represented by an agent in an action.[5]

In denying to certain parties full legal capacity, the praetor did not, indeed he could not, pronounce them *"infames,"* since the edict did not have the force of a statute, nor did the praetor have the power formally to curtail the civic honor of citizens. Gaius, however, in his Institutes which he composed after the middle of the second century declared: "Those whom the praetor places under such disabilities we call infamous."[6] These private writings of Gaius along with those of Papinianus (†212), Paulus (†ca. 235), Ulpianus (†228) and Modestinus (fl. 250) were given quasi-statutory force by Valentinian's Law of Citations in 426.[7]

It was from these sections of the praetorian edict as contained in Gaius that the compilers for Justinian in the sixth century took their list of cases of those with tarnished reputations and gave them the general name *"infames."*

These cases of infamy are all instances of *infamia iuris,* automatically incurred, or incurred after sentence. *"Infamia,"* the term, almost invariably refers to *infamia iuris* alone, though occasionally it may be extended to refer to what later came to be known as *infamia facti.* The term *"infamia facti"* came into use only at a much later time, though authors do indicate in their treatment of infamy that infamy of fact is involved to some extent at least in the Roman law.[9] Authors also see the equivalent of infamy of fact

---

[5] Sohm, *loc. cit.* This part of the *Edictum Perpetuum* of the praetors was later incorporated in the *Digest* of Justinian.—D. (3.1) 1, and the whole section on postulating was incorporated by Gratian into his *Decretum.*—c. 2, C. III, q. 7.

[6] *The Institutes of Gaius, Part I* (edited by De Zulueta, Oxford: Clarendon Press, 1946), IV, 182 pp. 304-305.

[7] Sohm, p. 118.

[8] As in D. (37.15) 2 and C. (12.1) 2.

[9] Azo, *Summa* (Lugduni, 1564), on C. (2.12), p. 23; Ionnes Andreae, *In Titulum de Regulis Iuris Novella Commentaria* (Venetiis, 1581), on reg. 87, *Liber Sextus Decretalium Bonifatii VIII,* p. 29; Donnellus, *Omnia Opera Commentariorum de Iure Civili* (12 vols., Macerata, Venetiis, 1831), V, bk. XVIII, cap. VI, n. 5; Gasparri, *Tractatus Canonicus de Sacra Ordinatione* (2 vols., Parisiis, Lugduni, 1893), I, 183 (hereafter cited: *De Sacra Ordinatione*).

expressed in the term *"turpitudo,"* as it is used in Roman law.[10] The close association of *infamia* and *turpitudo*, on the one hand, and the obvious distinction between them, on the other, do seem to be references to the two *infamiae* according to the distinction as it has come to be made.[11]

The medieval canonists found numerous instances of *infamia facti* in the *Digest* and *Codex* of Justinian. Most especially did they claim the presence of infamy of fact when the law itself explicitly decided that *infamia* (*iuris*) was not present.

This was true of the legal action known as the *condictio furtiva.*[12] The law stated: "Cessat ignominia in condictionibus quamvis ex famosis causis pendeant."[13] Although the law declared that *ignominia,* which was identified with *infamia,* was to cease in such actions, a *gravata opinio* concerning the defendant would continue to exist, the authors said.[14]

The negative indication of *infamia facti* was verified also in regard to interdicts, especially the interdict *"Unde vi,"* the glossators said.[15] The law pertinent to this matter was: "Neque 'Unde

---

[10] D'Angelo, *Ius Digestorum* (2 vols. in 4, Vol. I, pars I, Romae: Marietti, 1927), p. 279 (hereafter cited as D'Angelo); Amos, *The History and Principles of the Civil Law of Rome* (London, 1883), p. 111; Bernard, *The First Year of Roman Law* (New York City, 1906), p. 104; Sohm, p. 184.

[11] Thus C. (9.12) (8.2); C. (3.28) 27; C. (12.1) 2.

[12] The *condictio furtiva* was an action which the rightful owner alone could bring in a case of theft to regain the highest value the thing had since the theft, which action might be brought against the thief or his heir, though they were not at the time in possession of the thing stolen.—D. (12.1) 1; Buckland, p. 314; Leage, p. 366.

[13] D. (44.7) 36. The *"actiones famosae"* were those actions in which condemnation entailed infamy.—Sohm, p. 184. Cf. *infra,* p. 7.

[14] Cf. Ioannes Andreae, *loc. cit.;* Azo, *loc. cit.*

[15] Interdicts were the most important of the praetorian remedies. They were actions in ordinary form by the time of Justianian, and were classified as exhibitory, prohibitory, and restitutory. Restitutory interdicts ordered restoration of something or the undoing of some unlawful act. Of the several species, the appropriate restitutory interdict for the recovery of possession by a person who had been violently ejected from his lands or from a house was the interdictum *"Unde vi,"* and began with the words, "Unde vi tu illum deiecisiti. . . ."—Buckland, p. 412; Lee, p. 467.

vi,' neque aliud interdictum famosum est."[16] A person, then, against whom an interdict had been issued was not infamous by law. Since, however, an interdicted person was somewhat disgraced, the glossators said he was infamous by infamy of fact.[17]

Infamia facti was said to be incurred by one given an *interlocutio* or a reprimand by the judge or governor in the course of the trial. The law read: "Interlocutio praesidis, quae indicta est, infamem eum de quo quaeris fecisse non videtur . . ."[18]

The whipping of a defendant, when inflicted for the purpose of compelling him to tell the truth before the passing of a sentence, brought on not infamy of law but infamy of fact, the glossators said.[19]

The glossators also called infamous by infamy of fact those who were under accusation, and barred them from acting as attorneys,[20] and from prosecuting.[21]

The law itself, however, even prescinding from interpretations of later canonists, did distinguish from technical infamy that infamy recognizable by fact and public opinion, rather than by formal description. A response of the Emperor Alexander to Juventius in 230 A.D. made clear this reaction of people by declaring that

---

[16] D. (43.16) 13. To say that the interdict is not *"famosum,"* means that it does not carry with it an automatic stain of legal infamy.

[17] *Glossa ord.* ad D. (43.16) 13, *ad verbum "famosum."*

[18] C. (2.11) 19, *ad verbum "reformet."* That it was the judgment after the trial, and not the judgment during the trial, that rendered one infamous was also stated in the *Digest.*—D. (3.2) (13.6). The law stated, too, that the declaration by the judge of the accusation made in the introductory libellus caused some reproach, but did not induce *infamia* (*iuris*).—C. (2.11) 17. A decision of Papinian as incorporated in the *Digest* makes it seem that it had to be clear that the judge or the governor was inflicting *infamia* on someone, and not merely exhorting him, before infamy of the law rather than mere shame or infamy of fact was incurred by the person accused: "Ob haec verba sententiae praesidis provinciae, 'Callido commento videris accusatione instigator fuisse,' pudor potius oneratur, quam ignominia videtur irrogari; non enim qui exhortatur mandatoris opera fungitur." —D. (3.2) 20.

[19] C. (2.11) 14, *ad verbum "infamiam."*

[20] C. (2.12) 6.

[21] D. (48.1) 5, *ad verbum "amiserunt."*

adverse criticisms of a son in his father's will may bring about, not legal infamy, but its equivalent among good and serious men.[22]

An *infamia* induced through public opinion was also mentioned as the result of a condemnation to which *infamia* was not attached by law. In the Roman law the *"actiones famosae"* were those civil actions in which condemnation entailed infamy of law, and the actions which had such an effect were listed in the praetor's edict.[23] The law under consideration here said that, even though an action for fraud or injury was not an *actio famosa,* an infamy induced by public opinion was inevitable,[24] and for this reason filial devotion demanded that children or wards could not bring action for fraud or injury against their parents or guardians.[25]

The effects of infamy of fact in as far as it is adverted to in Roman law were: that a will could be set aside by brothers and sisters if a disreputable person was instituted an heir;[26] and notice could be taken of the fact of bad repute in making appointments to offices of honor,[27] in determining questions relating to the custody of one under age,[28] and in estimating the credibility or admissibility of a witness.[29]

---

[22] "Ea quae pater testamento suo filios increpans scripsit, infames quidem filios iure non faciunt, sed apud bonos et graves opinionem eius, qui patri displicuit, onerant."—C. (2.11) 13.

[23] Sohm, p. 184.

[24] ". . . re tamen ipsa et opinione hominum non effugiunt infamiae notam."

[25] D. (37.15) 2.

[26] "Fratres vel sorores uterini ab inofficiosi actione contra testamentum fratris vel sororis penitus arceantur; consanguinei autem, durante vel non agnatione contra testamentum fratris vel sororis de inofficioso quaestionem movere possunt, si scripti heredes infamiae vel turpitudinis vel levis notae macula adsparguntur."—C. (3.28) 27. Both the turpitude and slight stain (*"levis notae macula"*) are thought to indicate infamy of fact.—Amos, p. 111.

[27] "Neque famosis et notatis et quos scelus aut vitae turpitudo inquinat et quos infamia ab honestorum coetu segregat, dignitatis portae patebunt." —C. (12.1) 2. Cf. *Glossa ord.* ad D. (50.2) 3 and 12, and C. (2.11) 14, which laws dealt with the exclusion from the office of decurion of those who had been scourged.

[28] C. (9.43) 3.

[29] *Nov.* (90.1); D. (22.5) 3.

Article II. Infamy of Fact in the Early Church

Section 1. Infamy in the New Testament

The early Church was not so well developed as to need to adopt fully the Roman legal system, and with it the system of *infamia* as obtaining in Roman law. Yet, the concept of infamy of fact was not wanting in the Church even from its very beginnings. It is most evident in the Church's great solicitude for the good reputation required in candidates for the presbyterate and the episcopate. Thus, even in the first days of the Church, in order to provide for the needs of the Greek-speaking Christians, the Twelve instructed the disciples in the choice of the first deacons: "Therefore, brethren, select from among you seven men *of good reputation,* full of the Spirit and of wisdom, that we may put them in charge of this work."[30]

Saint Luke noted about Timothy that he was held in high regard by the Christians and thus qualified for the choice Saint Paul was to make of him as companion in the apostolic mission and for the episcopate. "And behold, a certain disciple was there named Timothy, son of a believing Jewess, but of a Gentile father. And he was highly thought of by the brethren in Lystra and Iconium."[31]

Later, in writing to Timothy, Paul was explicit in requiring a good name in candidates for Orders. Of those to be deacons, he said: "And let them first be tried and if found without reproach let them be allowed to serve."[32] One to be a bishop ". . . must have a good reputation with those who are outside, that he may not fall into disgrace and into a snare of the devil."[33] Moreover, to Titus, Paul said: "For a bishop must be blameless as being the steward of God, not proud, or ill-tempered, or a drinker, or a brawler, or

[30] Acts, 6, 3.

[31] Acts, 16, 1-2.

[32] I Tim., 3, 10.

[33] I Tim., 3, 7.

greedy for base gain; but hospitable, gentle, reserved, just, holy, continent. . . ."[34] And again, "A bishop must be blameless."[35]

There is nothing, however, to make us suppose that Saint Paul canonized the highly developed Roman system of *infamia.* Such a development within the Church did not come until centuries later. Infamy in the early Church, therefore, was infamy of fact.

Section 2. Infamy in the Non-inspired Sources

The solicitude of the Church for a blameless character in the ordinands was also witnessed in the non-inspired writings of the nascent Church. Thus in the *Didache* of the second century, the requisite characteristics for the *episcopi* and *diaconi* were spoken of: *"Eligite igitur, vobis episcopos et diaconos dignos Domino, viros mansuetos et argenti non cupidos et veraces et probatos."*[36]

Saint Clement of Rome, writing toward the end of the first century, made a good record stand in one's favor at a time of judgment.[37]

A good reputation was involved in the legislation concerning neophytes. In the Council of Elvira, held in 305 or 306, it was prescribed that the catechumenate of one with a good name last for two years, except in danger of death.[38] In such a case of danger of death, the same Council provided that any heathen with a good name might be baptized.[39]

The few times that *infamia* as such was mentioned in the ancient legislation of the Church, all seem to be instances of *infamia iuris.* Thus, canon 129 of a Council held in Carthage in 419, by which time the Church had become the official Church of the Empire, spoke of: "infamiae maculis aspersi, id est, histriones ac turpitudinibus subjectae personae, haeretici etiam, sive Pagani,

---

[34] Titus, 1, 7.

[35] I Tim., 3, 2.

[36] Kirch, *Enchiridion Fontium Historiae Ecclesiasticae Antiquae* (6. ed., quam curavit Leo Ueding, Barcelona: Editorial Herder, 1947), n. 6, p. 6 (hereafter cited as Kirch).

[37] Kirch, n. 13, p. 12.

[38] Hefele, *A History of the Christian Councils* (5 vols., T. & T. Clark, Vol. I, 2. ed., 1883, Vols. II-V, 1876-1896), I, 155 (hereafter cited as Hefele).

[39] Hefele, I, 152.

sive Judaei . . ," as being prohibited from accusing ecclesiastics.[40] While it is not perfectly clear that reference was made here to an *infamia iuris,* the refences to *infamia* made in the Councils held at Carthage in 421 and at Auxerre in 581 unmistakably pointed to *infamia iuris.*

Accordingly, the Church's very first legislation on infamy dealt with infamy of fact; however, when the term first came to be used in the Church's law, it was infamy of law, as we call it, which was understood.

Article III. Public Penance and Infamy of Fact

Public and solemn penance, as it existed in the Church especially from the third to the seventh centuries, always connoted the commission of a grave crime, e.g., adultery, apostasy, homicide, and accordingly involved defamation for one's character.[41] The

[40] Mansi, *Sacrorum Conciliorum Nova et Amplissima Collectio* (53 vols. in 60, Parisiis, 1901-1927), IV, 436 (hereafter cited as Mansi); Hefele, II, 290.

[41] The public penitential system in the Church from the time of Tertullian (160-222/3) till Gregory the Great (590-604) had the following characteristics. The sinner first asked to be admitted as a candidate for the Sacrament of Penance. When the request was granted by the Bishop, the penitent was clothed in a special penitential robe, and was directed to join the other penitents in public worship in a reserved part of the church. From that point of acceptance until his reconciliation, he was cut off from other Christians and formed part of an *ordo poenitentum* (". . . stent in ordine poenitentum,"—I Council of Orange (441), c. 3. Cf. Mansi, VI, pp. 436-437). According to the traditional accounts of public penance in the Western Church, the penitents were divided into four stations, sometimes called grades or classes. The first, the *flentes,* were really candidates for penance, great sinners who had to await their admission from outside the church. On being admitted they became *audientes,* apparently present at divine services until after the lessons and homily. After a certain time in that station, varying with the offense, the penitents passed into the grade of the *substrati,* so-called because they lay prostrate while the bishop, before excluding them, prayed over them and imposed hands on them. Finally, the *consistentes* were present during the whole service, but did not receive Communion.—Mortimer, *Origin of Primitive Penance in the Western Church* (Oxford: Clarendon Press, 1939), pp. 154-160; Beck, *The Pastoral Care of Souls in South East France During the Sixth Century* (Romae: Apud Aedes Universitatis Gregorianae, 1950), pp. 187-220 (hereafter cited as Beck).

relationship between infamy of fact and public penance has led authors to conclude that the Church's attitude toward infamy in these early centuries is to be gleaned from ecclesiastical legislation concerning the *poenitentes.*[42]

That the consequences of this type of "infamy" were at times severe is witnessed in Pope Leo's dealing with Rusticus in *Epistola 167.* The *poenitentes* were barred from ecclesiastical courts, were to avoid commercial transactions, were wholly forbidden to return to the army, and were ordinarily not to marry.[43]

The consequence, however, which received the most attention by far was the exclusion of the penitents from the clerical state. In the *Statuta Ecclesiae Antiquae,* it was decreed that a penitent regardless of how good he might be was not to be ordained. If the bishop had been ignorant of the fact that the one ordained was a penitent, the one ordained was to be deposed; if the bishop knowingly ordained one whom he knew to be a penitent, he was thenceforth to be deprived of the right to ordain.[44]

Pope Siricius (384-398) forbade the ordaining of penitents, and likewise forbade that clerics be subjected to public penance.[45]

The Council of Toledo (400), again forbidding the admission of *poenitentes* to the clerical state, made allowances for cases of necessity by permitting penitents to be admitted to the Orders of ostiariate and lectorate; they were not however, to read the epistles and the gospels.[46]

Innocent I in 404 declared that all *criminosi,* whether *poeni-*

---

[42] Phillips, *Du Droit Ecclésiastique dans ses Principes Généraux* (2. ed., traduit, revué et corrigée par Crouzet, 3 vols., Paris, 1855), I, 394 (hereafter cited as *Du Droit Ecclésiastique*) ; Gasparri, *De Sacra Ordinatione,* I, 113.

[43] *Bullarum Diplomatum et Privilegiorum Sanctorum Romanorum Pontificum Taurinensis Editio* (24 vols. et Appendix, Augustae Taurinorum, Neapoli, 1857-1872), I, 45.

[44] Bruns, *Canones Apostolorum et Conciliorum Saeculorum IV-VII* (2 vols., Berolini, 1839), I, 147 (hereafter cited as Bruns) ; c. 60, D. 50.

[45] Mansi, III, 660, n. 14; c. 66, D. 50.

[46] Bruns, I, n. 2, p. 204; c. 68, D. 50.

tentes or not, were prohibited from Holy Orders,[47] as he also did in an epistle to Agapitus.[48]

In 465 a Council of Rome, in canon 3, included the *poenitentes* among those who were to be considered irregular in regard to Holy Orders.[49] So, too, did Gelasius in the year 494.[50]

The Church in Gaul in the sixth century furnished extensive legislation on the *poenitentes* in regard to Orders. The Council of Agde in 506, in canon 43, declared that penitents were not to be ordained, and the ones already ordained were not to exercise their office. The Council called them *bigami,* perhaps an allusion to the *ordo* to which the penitents already belonged.[51] The same legislation was adopted at the Council of Epaon in Burgundy in 517,[52] and at the IV Council of Arles in 524.[53] The III Council of Orleans (538), in its canon 6, besides barring the *poenitentes* from Holy Orders, declared that a bishop who knowingly ordained such a one was to be suspended *ab officio* for six months, and the one ordained was to be deprived of his office permanently.[54]

The II Council of Braga (572) repeated, in canon 23, the legislation of the I Council of Toledo (400).[55] The IV Council of Toledo in 633 allowed one who had received penance in danger of death to become a cleric upon recovery, providing he merely

---

[47] Mansi, III, 1066; Jaffé, *Regesta Pontificum Romanorum ab condita Ecclesia ad annum post Christum natum MCXCV:II* (2. ed. by F. Kaltenbrunner ad annum 590, P. Ewald, 590-882, and S. Loewenfeld, 882-1198, and also referred to as JK, JE, and JL, Lipsiae, 1885-1888), JK, n. 292; c. 1, D. 51.

[48] Mansi, III, 1032. This in part was included by Gratian in his *Decretum,* c. 60, D. 50, occasioning this remark by Gratian himself, "Hoc non de quibuslibet poenitentibus intelligitur, sed de illis tantum, qui post penitenciam saecularis militiae cingulum accipiunt."

[49] Mansi, VII, 961; Hefele, IV, 15.

[50] Mansi, VIII, 37; c. 59, D. 50; also c. 1, D. 55.

[51] Bruns, II, 154; cf. supra, p. 10, note 41.

[52] Bruns, II, 167.

[53] Bruns, II, 175; *Monumenta Germaniae Historica* (Hanoveriae, 1826-), Legum Sectio III, *Concilia*, I, *Concilia Aevi Merovingici,* p. 37 (hereafter cited as *MGH*).

[54] Mansi, IX, 14; *MGH, Concilia,* I, 75.

[55] Bruns, II, 49.

declare himself a sinner apart from the need of openly confessing a crime.[56]

Public penance was on the wane in the seventh century. Seventh century France where legislation on public penance had been so thorough the century before, certainly saw the adoption of private auricular confession on an imposing scale.[57]

Yet Gratian (†ca. 1157) included much of the earlier legislation on public penance in his *Decretum* in the twelfth century,[58] and Raymond of Peñafort (1175-1275) explained public penance as an irregularity to Orders.[59]

Article IV. Infamy of Fact in the Pseudo-Isidorian Decretals[60]

Section 1. Infamy of Fact in the Capitularies

Before dealing with the Pseudo-Isidorian Decretals in detail, one must consider an earlier collection, the *Capitularies of Ansegisus,* written in the same century (a. 827), which served as a source book for the Pseudo-Isidorian compiler-authors. It was a

---

[56] Mansi, X, 631.

[57] Beck, p. 220.

[58] Canons 59, 60, 66, 68, D. L; C. 1, D. LI; c. 1, D. LV; c. 1, D. XXXVI; c. 17, C. VI, q. 1.

[59] Raymond of Peñaford, *Summa Iuris* [to be distinguished from the famous *Summa de Casibus* of St. Raymond], (edited by Msgr. J. Serra, Barcelona, 1945), p. 83.

[60] The collection known as the Pseudo-Isidorian Decretals was a clever falsification of the *Collectio Hispana* of the sixth century. This spurious collection with its false documents, interpolations, forgeries and alterations is of unknown authorship. However, the collection of the decretals seems to have been part of a program devised by a group who parcelled out the work that produced actually several collections. The fourth and main collection was produced sometime between 845 and 852.—Cicognani, *Canon Law* (2. ed., Reprint, Westminster, Md.: Newman Press, 1949), pp. 235-248 (hereafter cited as Cicognani).

This spurious collection of the ninth century had as its *raison d'être* the increase of power of the local ordinary against the nobility, the metropolitan and the lower clergy. With this purpose in mind, the compiler-authors included the concept of *infamia facti* in the stringent legislation concerning who might accuse a bishop or a cleric.

collection in four books of the *Capitularies* of the Frankish Kings. This collection contained only genuine documents.[61]

Under the title, "Concerning the type of persons not allowed to judge, accuse or give testimony," the compiler included not only the *infames,* but also the *viles personae.*[62] The *infames* he mentioned seemed to be those who were such by infamy of law; the *viles personae* more likely were those who were infamous in fact.

Likewise those, ". . . qui non sunt bonae conversationis et eorum vita est accusabilis . . .," were not to accuse bishops and noblemen.[63]

Section 2. Infamy of Fact in the Capitula Angilramni

This spurious collection, with which Bishop Angilramnus actually had no connection, made use of the spurious collection of Benedict the Deacon. This latter collection used as a source the *Capitularies of Ansegisus,* which for the most part were authentic.[64]

The terms "infamia" and "infames" in Angilramnus and throughout the Pseudo-Isidorian decretals in general pertained to *infamia iuris.*[65]

References to infamy of fact as we know it, however, are

---

[61] Cicognani, p. 237.

[62] Hoc sancimus, ut in palatiis nostris ad accusandum et iudicandum et testimonium faciendum non se exhibeant viles personae et infames, histriones scilicet, nugatores, manzeres, scurrae, concubinarii, neque ex turpium feminarum commixtione progeniti aut servi aut criminosi. Frequenter enim homines huiusmodi ex suspicione conversationis pravae et naturae, ut inferiores non videantur, quod placet asserere nituntur contra digniores."—*MGH,* Legum Sectio II *Capitularia,* Tomus I, *Capitularia Regum Francorum* (ed. A. Boretius, Hannoverae, 1883) Pars I, p. 334, *Capitula Hludowico vel Hlothario Adscripta,* n. 167—*Capitula Francica,* cap. 8.

[63] *Ibid.,* p. 400, *Ansegisi Capitularium,* cap. 35.

[64] Cicognani, pp. 237-239; Hinschius, *Decretales Pseudo-Isidorianae et Capitula Angilramni* (Lipsiae, 1863), p. clxxii (hereafter cited as Hinschius).

[65] Citations which from their very context prove this are numerous; such canons from Pseudo-Isidore as appear in Gratian are: c. 1, C. II, q. 3; c. 2, C. II, q. 4; cc. 18, 23, 39, C. II, q. 7; cc. 3, 4, 8, 9, 11, C. III, q. 4; cc. 6, 9, 11, C. III, q. 5; c. 23, C. III, q. 7; cc. 2, 3, 8, 17, C. VI, q. 5; c. 1, C. V, q. 6; c. 2, C. XXXV, q. 2.

discernible in such expressions as "qui . . . non rectae conversationis,"[66] and ". . . hi qui non sunt bonae conversationis."[67] To determine those who were not well-spoken of, an investigation was prescribed before these could be admitted to court.[68] There was a distinction between this infamy and infamy strictly so-called. Thus, for bringing a case into court, it was said: ". . . ad hoc admitti non debent, nisi bonae conversationis et rectae fidei viri et hi qui omni suspicione careant et bonae vitae clareant, neque infames existant."[69]

Section 3. Infamy of Fact in the Pseudo-Isidorian Decretals

Again, where the terms *"infamia"* or *"infames"* were used, they were used in reference to those who were infamous by law.[70] For infamy of fact, one must appeal to expressions similar to those in Angilramnus: ". . . a vilibus et reprobis et non idoneis personis infamari noluit . . ."; "qui non sunt rectae fidei et conversationis . . ."; ". . . qui docuerit se irreprehensibilem fidem ac conversationem ducere . . ."; ". . . qui non sunt bonae conversationis. . . ."[71]

All these expressions here referred to are contained in laws which deal with the exclusion of those with a bad reputation from the prerogative of making a formal accusation or of acting in court.

In these false Decretals there sometimes is made a distinction between the *infames* and those whose names are not respected in conversation. Thus Pelagius II (579-590) is credited with saying:

> Canonica sanctorum patrum statuta sequentes, ac roborantes, omnes infames, et eorum qui non sunt eorum gentis, vel quorum fides, vita, et libertas nescitur, et qui non sunt bonae conversationis, vel quorum vita est accusabilis, ab omni accusatione

[66] *Capitula Angilramni*—Hinschius, n. 3, p. 758.

[67] *Ibid.*, p. 761.

[68] *Ibid.*, p. 758; n. 12, p. 761; n. 4, p. 759.

[69] Hinschius, p. 759, n. 4.

[70] *Ibid.*, n. 18, p. 229—c. 9, C. III q. 5; p. 96—c. 9, C. III, q. 4; p. 164—c 17, C. VI, q. 1.

[71] Hinschius, pp. 26, 140, 114, 730.

episcoporum funditus submovemus. Similiter et omnes, quos divinae leges mortuos appellant, submovendos esse ab eadem accusatione, et publicae poenitentiae submittendos iudicamus.[72]

So, too, Pope Damasus (366-384) was reported to have written that witnesses were to be without infamy, and beyond suspicion, and blameless.[73] Rufinus (†1190) when commenting on this at a much later period in history noted that it was the *infamia iuris* which was explicitly mentioned in this canon.[74]

Article V. Infamy of Fact in the *Decretum Gratiani* and in the *Decretales*.[45]

Section 1. The General Concept of Infamy of Fact in the Decretum and in the Decretales

Since the *Decretum* and the *Decretales* were compilations of former legislation, and since that legislation did not deal with infamy of fact directly, no explicit references to infamy of fact are found in these collections. There are, however, those who feel that often the *infamia* which receives mention in the laws of these collections applies to both infamy of law and infamy of fact.[76] The basis for this seems traceable to the glosses rather than to the laws

[72] Hinschius, p 730; c. 6, C. III, q. 5.

[73] Hinschius, p. 503; c. 39, C. II, q. 7.

[74] *Die Summa Decretorum* (edited by H. Singer, Paderborn, 1902), p. 187, on c. 39, C. 11, q. 7 (hereafter cited as *Summa*).

[75] Gratian, a Camaldolese monk, published in approximately 1140 his *Decretum*, a compilation of previous laws drawn up from the writings of the popes, and the general and particular councils and synods of the Church. In order to bring together into one collection the various decretal letters written by the popes in the years following the publication of the *Decretum*, and likewise to give them the force of universal law, Gregory IX (1227-1241) entrusted to St. Raymond of Peñafort the task of compiling what has come to be known as the *Decretales Gregorii IX*. These with other collections of decretals by later pontiffs, along with the *Decretum* of Gratian, together formed the *Corpus Iuris Canonici*, and thus existed as a practical norm of law.—Cicognani, pp. 273-321.

[76] Gasparri, *De Sacra Ordinatione*, I, 196; Phillips, *Du Droit Ecclésiastique*, I, 393.

themselves, for it is in the comments of the glossators that one finds for the first time the use of the term *"infamia facti."* These glossators felt that in the Roman law and also in the ecclesiastical law there was implied a certain type of infamy of fact. Accordingly, in considering the development of the notion of infamy of fact in canon law, one must study the writings of these glossators and of those who commented on the *Decretum* and the *Decretales,* particularly those of Gregory IX's collection, namely, the decretists and the decretalists.[77]

The inclusion of *infamia facti* within the comprehension of the meaning of the word *infamia* as used in the earlier laws is clear in one gloss especially, where it is said, "Infamia alia iuris: alia facti . . . sed haec distinctio non videtur habere locum secundum canones; cum omne mortale crimen infamet. . . ."[78] The distinction, however, was generally made,. and when *infamia* applied to both infamy of fact and of law, it was noted in the gloss.[79] The distinction is explicit in one particular gloss, which explained that there is an infamy inflicted by way of sentence or sustained automatically for certain violations of the law, that there is also another infamy called infamy of fact or defamation (*infamatio*), removable by way of canonical purgation, and that there is a third type of infamy, called canonical infamy, which overtakes anyone who has committed mortal sin, and is set aside by way of penance.[80] This identi-

[77] The glossators here spoken of were students of the law who, beginning in the eleventh and the twelfth centuries, made explanatory interpretations of the law on the sides of the pages, or between the lines of the texts of the laws. The *decretists* were those students of the law who continued Gratian's work of studying the old canons, using Gratian's *Decretum* as their text. The *decretalists* commented on the law as contained in the collections of the papal letters.

[78] *Glossa ord. ad* c. 2, C. III, q. 7, *ad verbum "infamia."*

[79] *Glossa ord. ad* c. 5, D. LI, *ad verbum "infamiae."*

[80] "Discunt tamen quidam, quod infamia, quae est irrogata per sententiam, vel quae contrahitur ipso facto, ut cum aliqua deprehenditur in adulterio, vel cum aliquis contrahit binas nuptias . . . haec infamia non purgatur per quamcumque poenitentiam. . . . Alia est infamia facti, et melius dicitur infamatio quae inducit purgationem, et illa aboletur purgatione praestita. . . . Est etiam quaedam infamia canonica, quae irrogatur ex quolibet peccato mortali . . . et aboletur per poenitentiam. . . ." *Glossa ord. ad* c. 2, C. VI, q. 1, *ad verbum "leges."*

fication of *infamia facti* and *infamatio* is in a sense the key to the understanding of the specific meaning which the glossators and decretists and decretalists attached to the expression *"infamia facti."* A slight distinction between the two terms, as made by the author Henricus Boich (1310-1350), was based on Ioannes Andreae's commentary. According to this distinction the accusation of crime was the *proximate* cause of the infamy, whereas it was but the *remote* cause of the defamation or *infamatio;* some such thing as incarceration could be the proximate cause of the latter.[81]

Section 2. Infamy of Fact and Canonical Purgation

In Gratian's *Decretum* and especially in the Decretals of Gregory IX, *purgatio canonica* was consistently considered as a means for removing infamy of fact.[82]

To appreciate fully the concept of infamy of fact as it was understood at the time of these collections, it is necessary to realize the nature and purpose of canonical purgation. *Purgatio canonica* was a proof of innocence by one who had been defamed, i.e., accused of crime. This proof was to be achieved through the solemn taking of an oath along with the deposition in favor of the one accused by a certain number of witnesses beyond reproach who judged in good conscience and swore that the individual was innocent of that of which he was accused.[83] The required number of witnesses

---

[81] H. Boich, *In Quinque Decretalium Libros Commentaria* (2 vols. in 1, Venetiis, 1576), Vol. II, p. 269, n. 18 (hereafter cited as Boich), *ad c.* 54, X, *de testibus et attestationibus,* II, 20.

[82] Cc. 6-19, C. II, q. 5; c. 13, X, *de simonia ne aliquid pro spiritualibus exiguatur vel promittatur,* V, 3; c. 19, X, *de accusationibus, inquisitionibus et denunciationibus,* V, 1; c. 5, X, *de adulteriis et stupro,* V, 16; cc. 4, 5, 6, 8, 10, 12, 14, *de purgatione canonica,* V 34.

[83] Hostiensis, *Summa Aurea* (Lugduni, 1568), pp. 396-397; Innocentius IV (Sinibaldus de Fieschi), *In Quinque Libros Decretalium Commentaria* (Venetiis, 1570), pp. 641-644; Panormitanus, *Commentaria In Quinque Libros Decretalium* (5 vols. in 8, Vol. VI, *In Quartum et Quintum Librum Decretalium Commentaria,* Venetiis, 1588), pp. 312-322 (hereafter cited as *Commentaria*); Schmalzgrueber, *Ius Ecclesiasticum Universum* (5 vols. in 7, Parisiis, 1864-1870), VI, pp. 537-540 (hereafter cited as *Ius Canonicum*); Phillips, *Compendium Iuris Ecclesiastici* (3. ed., 1. ed. Latinae versionis, Ratisbonae, 1875), pp. 339-340; Wernz-Vidal, *Ius Canonicum ad Codicis*

varied from time to time, and from case to case, but eventually this was a discretional matter left to the judge.[84] Though the origin of purgation in canonical legislation is not definite, there are several references to it in the Register of Gregory in such wise as to indicate a usage of long standing by the sixth century.[85]

The purgations took different forms. The three mentioned in the Register of Letters of Gregory the Great were performed before relics of the Saints. A very different means, however, was indicated by the Council of Worms in the year 868. This Council set down the law that the purgation was to be accomplished through the reception of the Eucharist in the event that a theft was charged against monks in monasteries. The monks were to assemble for Mass celebrated by the abbot or by one of the monks, and they were to receive Communion in proof of their innocence according to the form, "Corpus Domini sit tibi ad probationem hodie."[86]

Normam Exactum (7 vols. in 8, Romae: Apud Aedes Universitatis Gregorianae, Vol. II, 3. ed., 1943, Vol. IV, Pars I, 1934, Vol. IV, 1927-1928), VI, 670-671 (hereafter cited as *Ius Canonicum*).

[84] *Glossa ord., ad c.* 13, X, *de simonia ne aliquid pro spiritualibus exiguatur vel promittatur,* V, 3, *ad verba "quinta vel sexta manu";* cc. 1, 5, 10, X, *de purgatione canonica,* V, 34.

[85] *MGH, Gregorii Papae Registri Epistolarum* Libri I-VII, Lib. II, ep. 30, *Epistolarum* Tomus I (edd. P. Ewald et P. Ewald et L.M. Hartmann, Berolini, 1891), p. 126—which letter to the Pretor of Sicily, Justin, in July, 592, commended Bishop Leo of Catania for having purged himself of certain crimes concerning which a *"sinister rumor"* had been circulated with the Bishop as the target. In spite of the fact that the Pope had found him guiltless, it was felt that there was need of purgation to protect his reputation. This legislation was included by Gratian in the *Decretum* (c. 7, C. II, q. 5), as were two other canons taken from Gregory: *MGH, Gregorii Papae Registri Epistolarum* Libri VIII-IX, Lib. IX, ep. 178, *Epistolarum* Tomus II, Pars I (edd. P. Ewald et L.M. Hartmann, Berolini, 1893), p. 173—(c. 7, C. II, q. 5); *MGH, Gregorii Papae Registri Epistolarum* Libri X-XIV, Lib. XIII, ep. 7, *Epistolarum* Tom. II, Pars I (edd. P. Ewald et L.M. Hartmann, Berolini, 1893), p. 372—(c. 8, C. II, q. 5).

[86] *Collectio Conciliorum Germaniae* (10 vols. et Index, Coloniae Augustae Agrippinensium, 1759-1790, Vols. I-V, ed. cura J. F. Schannat—Jos. Hartzheim, 1759-1763; Vols. VI-VII, ed. cura H. Scholl, 1765-1769; Vols. IX-X, ed. cura A. Neissen, 1771-1775; Index ed. cura A. J. Heselmann, 1790), II, 313; c. 23, C. II, q. 5.

A purgation through such a means is to be distinguished from the *purgatio vulgaris,* a pagan institute (which, however, was adopted to a certain extent by the Church after the barbarian invasions), whereby a man "proved" his innocence through certain feats of physical endeavor, e.g., by enduring the test of cold water, by defying the torment of hot irons, or by engaging in a duel.[87]

A strict prohibition against this "proof" of innocence through ordeals was contained in a letter of Pope Alexander II (1061-1073) to Bishop Rainaldo of Como in the year 1063.[88]

Subsequent Pontiffs repeated this condemnation of the *purgatio vulgaris.* Thus Coelestine III (1181-1198), Innocent III (1198-1216), in a letter of March 22, 1203,[89] and Honorius III (1216-1227), in a letter of Dec. 30, 1222[90] all forbade the employment of this purgation in proof of innocence. With the condemnations of the *purgatio vulgaris* as contained in these three letters Raymond of Peñafort formed the thirty-fifth title, *De Purgatione Vulgari,* of Book V in the Decretals of Gregory IX.

Canonical purgation was, then, the Church's way in which a man when accused of a crime could prove the falsehood of the accusation raised against him and thus prove his innocence.[91]

---

[87] Simpsos-Stone make mention of the following ordeals which were in use among the Germanic Christians around the year 800: 1) the judgment of the glowing iron; 2) the judgment of the plowshares (over which the accused walked with bare feet); 3) the judgment of boiling water; 4) the test of cold water; 5) the judgment of the morsel (a large wad of bread and cheese, which the accused had to swallow whole).—*Cases and Readings on Law and Society in Three Books,* Book I, *Law and Society in Evolution,* American Casebook Series (St. Paul, Minn.: West Publishing Co., 1948), pp. 303-306.

[88] "Vulgarem [purgationem] . . ., ac nulla canonica sanctione fultam legem, serventis scilicet sive frigidae aquae, ignitique ferri contactum, aut cuiuslibet popularis inventionis (quia farbricante hec sunt omnino ficta invidia), nec ipsum exhibere, nec aliquo te modo volumus postulare, imo apostolica auctoritate prohibemus firmissime."—Mansi, XIX, 984.

[89] Potthast, *Regesta Pontificum Romanorum inde ab anno post Christum natum* 1198 *ad annum 1304* (2 vols., Berolini, 1874-1875), I, n. 1865, p. 163.

[90] Potthast, *op. cit.,* I, n. 6910, p. 599.

[91] ". . . per purgationem demonstratur infamiam sive accusationem fuisse falsam . . ."—Guido a Baisio, *Commentaria in Decretorum Volumen*

The term *"infamia facti"* was applied to what resulted from a false accusation. This was made even more obvious by a gloss[92] which made mention of another canon, presenting it as the foremost example of *infamia facti.* The canon to which reference was made, a portion of an epistle of St. Gregory, points out that God permits detractions and reproofs against the *good* in order to effect a proper balance to the excessive praise which may jeopardize Christian humility.[93]

To take the oath implied innocence, the regaining of good repute, and at times even the restoring of one's office; not to take it meant that a condemnation, or the deprivation of one's benefice or office, was to follow, as if the person were already convicted.[94] Even so, purgation was employed only in the event that there was not available any other proof of innocence.[95] It was invoked only when the infamy was public and notorious, regardless of whether or not the crime of which the person was accused was public in nature.[96] Either the prescribed forms of canonical purgation,[97] or the rules of the religious institute, were to be followed.[98]

The qualities of the *compurgatores,* i.e., of those who took the oath together with and in defense of the defamed person (*infamatus*) were also specified in law. They were to be honest, well-thought of individuals, not apt to perjure themselves out of prejudice or for the sake of money, but well acquainted with the

---

(Venetiis, 1577), p. 142; "Canonica purgatio est nocentis infamiae ecclesiasticae innocentiae canonicae facta detectio."—Hostiensis, p. 396, *ad titulum* 34, X, *de purgatione canonica,* V, 34.

[92] *Supra,* p. 17, note 80; *glossa ord. ad* c. 2, C. VI, q. 1, *ad verbum "leges".*

[93] "Sunt plurimi, qui vitam bonorum amplius quam debent, laudant: et ne qua elatio de laude surrepat, permittit omnipotens Deus malos in obtrectationem, et obiurgationem prorumpere, ut si qua culpa ab ore vituperantium suffocetur. Hinc est ergo quod doctor Gentium se in praedicatione currere testatur per infamiam, et bonam famam, qui etiam dicit ut seductores, et veraces.—c. 11, C. VI, q. 1.

[94] Cc. 4, 7, X, *de purgatione canonica,* V, 34.

[95] *Eod. tit., passim.*

[96] C. 13, X, *de simonia ne aliquid pro spiritualibus exiguatur vel promittatur,* V, 3.

[97] C. 5, X, *de purgatione canonica,* V, 34; c. 17, C. II, q. 5.

[98] C. 3, *eod. tit.*

accused and with his way of life.[99] It sufficed that they be *"tolerati ab ecclesia,"* not condemned for any crime, and it was required that they swear to the truth.[100]

Canonical purgation was employed for the removal of a harmful *infamia facti,* and not simply for the removal of the cause for suspicion which some evil-minded persons entertained. Thus, at times there were no accusers at all, for even when all accusers had desisted from their allegations against the one defamed, the latter nevertheless had to swear to his innocence, undoubtedly for the allaying of every threat of scandal.[101] In certain cases, namely when the infamy was public a bishop could even force a clergyman of his diocese to purge himself of some false accusation, though there were no accusers or witnesses at all.[102] On the other hand, if there were witnesses who could testify, then *purgatio* was inadmissible.

For the protection of the *infamatus,* his accusers were also called upon at times to take the oath of purgation in proof of their truthfulness in the manner of a "wager of law."[103]

To warrant the procedure of purgation, there was need simply of a defamation *"apud bonos et graves,"* even though they were not the accusers.[104] This had always been basic to the notion of *infamia facti,* even from what is perhaps the first mention of infamy of fact in Roman law.[105] The glossator however, in commenting on the above-mentioned canon in the Decretals, posed this problem: If the infamy which arose among some unsavory individuals later obtained among the good and serious-minded, did such infamy

---

[99] C. 7, X, *de purgatione canonica,* V, 34.

[100] Cc. 9, 13; and *glossa ord. ad* c. 5, *eod. tit., ad verbum "credunt."*

[101] *Casus ad* c. 3, *eod. tit.*

[102] C. 6, *eod tit.* A gloss to the canon stated that the bishop could force the priest in such cases wherein the public infamy pointed to crimes such as incest, heresy or adultery (*ad verbum "deficientibus"*); and a just cause was required for an appeal, e.g. ". . . quando excedit modum episcopus in purgatione vel alias eum gravat. . . ." (*ad verbum "appelaverit"*).

[103] Cc. 2, 5, *eod. tit.*

[104] ". . . Si vero nullus apparuerit legitimus accusator, et ipsum inveneritis apud bonos et graves super praedictis criminibus, vel ipsorum altero infamatum, purgationem ei canonicam indicatis. . . ."—c. 15, *eod. tit.*

[105] C. (2.11) 13; cf. *supra,* p. 7, note 22.

call for the procedure of purgation?[106] The glossator himself, it is seen, felt that such infamy demanded a procedure of purgation for the removal of any threatened scandal. The citations he gave on their face favor the other view, namely, that the family had to originate as well as exist among good and respectable people, but the glossator maintained that these citations were not irreconcilable with his own view.[107] In accord with the cited texts, Panormitanus (1386-1453) seemed to favor the view that infamy had to originate among the good in order to demand purgation, for he taught that infamy when arising among those who are jealous of the *infamatus* does not prevent the latter from being advanced to some dignity: "Infamia facti habens ortum ab aemulis non impediat quem promovendum ad dignitatem. . . ."[108] And again: ". . . Quando constat infamiam processisse ab aemulis, non est ex ea indicenda purgatio etiam ad instantiam aliorum, nec debet iudex commoveri ex tali infamia contra infamatum."[109] A gloss, however, to a canon already cited in favor of the view to which Panormitanus seemed to adhere states that a purgation had to be undergone no matter what the origin of the infamy might be, in view of the scandal that was involved. The deacon in the case contended that the infamy had arisen from those whom he termed *aemuli,* but the Pope in his response pointed out that the *publica nota* is the essential mark of infamy and accordingly he demanded a procedure of purgation.[110] Hostiensis († 1271) subscribed to

---

[106] "Notatur quod dicit apud bonos et graves fuerit infamatus: per hoc videtur quod non refert undecumque orta fuerit infamia, ex quo apud tales iam laborat, sufficit ad purgationem indicendam. . . . Dicunt quidem, quod si infamia orta sit a vilibus et aemulis non compellitur ad purgationem. Alii dicunt (quod videtur verius) quod ex quo aliquis infamatus est apud bonos et graves, compelli debet ad purgationem, ne apud illos incredibilis remaneat post iura inducta."—*glossa ad* c. 15, *eod. tit., ad verba "apud bonos et graves."*

[107] C. 52, C. XI, q. 3; c. 19, C. II, q. 5; c. 24, X, *de accusationibus, inquisitionibus et denunciationibus,* V, 1.

[108] *Commentaria,* VII, 318, ad c. 12, X, *de purgatione canonica,* V, 34.

[109] *Loc. cit.*

[110] ". . . satis potest dici quod indicenda est purgatio undecumque procedat infamia, saltem propter scandalum. . . ."—*glossa ord. ad* c. 24, X, *de accusationibus, inquisitionibus et denunciationibus,* V, 1, *ad verba "a male-*

the view that, if infamy obtained among the good and serious-minded, it warranted the procedure of purgation, even though it had originated among the malicious.[111]

Besides postulating truthfulness, respectability and serious thinking on the part of those with whom a person was regarded as infamous, the law further required that with regard to the number there had to be more than just a few.[112] Boich declared that if the testimony of a few people who were beyond reproach brought defamation to anyone, a defense was warranted for the person thus defamed. The sworn testimony of two or three would then suffice for the vindication of the defendant.[113] Guido a Baisio († 1313) maintained that even if many witnesses were responsible for the defamation of anyone, but the common opinion was in the man's favor, then it was the common opinion that was to be preferred in the settlement of the case in hand.[114]

Section 3. Effects of Infamy of Fact in the Decretum and in the Decretales

Once again it is to be noted that direct legislation on persons infamous by reason of infamy of fact is lacking in the *Decretum* and in the *Decretales*, and that the *dicta* of the glossators are accordingly important for the consideration that is to be given to this matter of infamy. The following limitations were placed on persons infamous by reason of infamy of fact:

a) They could not bring an action in court, nor could they serve as lawyers.

---

volis," which gloss cites c. 14, X, *de purgatione canonica,* V, 34. This latter canon forbade (indirectly) a bishop from ordaining a certain deacon T., who wished to be ordained, but concerning whom it was said by those who were jealous of him that he was the son of a priest; if the infamy was public and no proof against it was available, the deacon was to purge himself and then be admitted to ordination.

[111] *Summa Aurea,* p. 396, on c. 16, X, *de purgatione canonica,* V, 34.

[112] "Qui iudex propter dicta paucorum eum infamatum reputare non debet, cuius apud bonos et graves laesa opinio non existit."—c. 21, X, *de accusationibus, inquisitionibus et denunciationibus,* V, 1, *in fine.*

[113] *In Quinque Decretalium Libros Commentaria,* II, 95, n. 6, on c. 22, X, *de testibus et attestationibus,* II, 20.

[114] *Commentaria in Decretorum Volumen,* p. 143, paragraph 2.

b) They could not be promoted to honors, nor could they receive orders.

c) They could not testify.

d) They were at times liable to suspension, and deprivation of office or benefice.

A) Those who were infamous could not level judicial accusations against others. One accused could not be a legitimate accuser.[115] The rubric to this same canon stated that this inability to accuse obtained *"in iudicio."* The same law held in Gratian's *Decretum.*[116] The decretist Rufinus († 1190) made it clear that it was infamy of fact as well as infamy of law that prevented one from testifying.[117]

Furthermore, one who was infamous could not be an advocate or a lawyer.[118] A special warning to bishops appeared in the canon which demanded that they be represented in matters ecclesiastical and personal as well by advocates with good reputations.[119]

---

[115] "Si legitimus non fuerit accusator, non fatigetur accusatus."—c. 1, X, *de accusationibus, etc.,* V, 1. In explanation of this canon, the glossator said, ". . . Debet enim esse sine crimine, non inimicus, bonae famae et opinionis, qui alium accusat, alias non est legitimus accusator." In a memnonic which listed those who are excluded from accusing, he included the *"infamis."*

Hoc non accusant, quos nostra sequentia signant:
Foemina, pupillus, delatus, crimine tentus,
Suspectus, quaestus, corruptus, sortilegusque,
Infamis, servus, pauper, cum milite princeps,
Libertus, socius socium nec non inimici,
Clericus ecclesiam, nullus deferre valebit.—*ad verbum "legitimus."*

[116] C. 39, C. II, q. 7; c. 8, C. III, q. 5, besides the many canons of Pseudo-Isidore treated above, pp. 13-16.

[117] *Summa,* p. 187, on c. 39, C. II, q. 7.

[118] C. 2, C. III, q. 7.

[119] "Quia episcopus universique sacerdotes ad solam laudem Dei bonorumque operum actionem constituuntur, debet unusquisque eorum tam pro ecclesiasticis, quam etiam pro suis actionibus (excepto publico videlicet crimine) habere advocatum non malae famae suspectum, sed bonae opinionis, et laudabilis artis inventum, ne dum humana lucra attendunt, eterna premia perdant."—c. 3, C. V, q. 3.

In regard to bishops, Rufinus said that, though the *infames* could not ordinarily accuse them, there were certain exceptions to that rule, in crimes of simony, of heresy, and of insurrection against the supreme authority of the king.[120]

B) Those who were infamous could not be promoted to honors; one against whom strong accusations had been made was not be honored.[121]

Nor could infamous persons be promoted to Holy Orders.[122] Pope Gregory the Great, however, in a letter to a bishop Venantius, declared that a certain priest who had been suspended from the exercise of his Orders might very well continue to act as procurator for the monastery. The glossator when discussing this provision of the law, which was incorporated as a canon in the *Decretum Gratiani,* explained that the infamous were barred from honors, not jobs. Besides, he said, no great perfection was required in a procurator.[123] He could not serve as procurator for the bishop, the same gloss stated. The bishop was to surround himself with priests of good reputation at all times.[124]

C) Those who were infamous by reason of infamy of fact were barred from testifying in a criminal case. The ones thought to be so restricted by law were those who were accused of a crime themselves, *pendente accusatione,"* i.e., until they had proved their own innocence.[125] The gloss to the canon explained:

---

[120] *Summa,* p. 281.

[121] C. 4, X, *de accusationibus, inquisitionibus et denunciationibus,* V, 1. The glossator explains about this law which is: "Valde grave est ut vir de quo tanta et talia denunciantur (cum ante requiri et discuti debeant) honoretur."—"Dicitur hic, quod si aliquis infamatur, non debet ad honores promoveri, donec de hoc inquiratur, vel inde se purgaverit. Notetur quod opinio promovendi ad honores vacillare non debet, et sic, pendente accusatione, promoveri non debet."—*ad Casus.*

[122] C. 14, X, *de purgatione canonica,* V, 34; c. 56, X, *de testibus et attestationibus,* II, 20; *glossa ad* c. 16, X, *de purgatione canonica,* V, 34;—*ad verbum "postquam"*; c. 8, D. LXXVII; *glossa ad* c. 5, D. LI—*ad verbum "infamiae."*

[123] C. 10, D. L, and *glossa ad verbum "solicitudinem."*

[124] C. 60, C. II, q. 7: "Episcopi . . . semper secum presbiteros et diaconos, aut alios boni testamenti clericos habeant. . . ."

[125] C. 56, X, *de testibus et attestationibus,* II, 20.

> Note that when anyone is accused of a crime, his reputation is immediately worsened; accordingly he cannot be admitted to testify in criminal cases . . . since witnesses must be beyond suspicion, and without infamy.[126]

Once cleared of any guilt and freed from infamy, one was not to be barred from testifying even in a criminal case in a civil court. If a person was convicted of the crime of which he had been accused, or if he confessed, his testimony could be prohibited in a criminal case, regardless of whether or not he had done penance. His testimony was, however, allowed in a civil case.[127] There was, however, contained in this canon the following provision: if after one had been accused and then later cleared of guilt, a *"gravata opinio"* concerning that person continued to obtain he could be prohibited from testifying in a criminal case. This provision apparently stood in opposition to the whole theory regarding the *infamia facti* and the *purgatio canonica* of the period under discussion. Accordingly, the authors of the time in discussing the matter asked: What kind of infamy is it that prohibits a man from testifying after he has proved himself innocent of some accusation leveled against him? Panormitanus (1384-1453) reported the authors' doctrine under four separate viewpoints.[128]

1) Hostiensis († 1271), Petrus de Sampsone († after 1260), and Bernardus de Monte Mirato († 1296) (cited as "Abbas Antiquus") concluded that the infamy must be an *infamia iuris*.

2) Ioannes Andreae († 1348), distinguishing between *"infamia facti"* and *"infamatio,"* maintained that *infamia facti* came as the effect of being accused of crime, and that *infamia* or *aggravatio opinionis* resulted from such a blot on character as was occasioned by incarceration. In the canon under discussion, it was not *infamia facti* in the strict sense, but rather this latter *aggravatio opinionis* which prevented one from testifying in a criminal case. Even in a

---

[126] *Glossa ord.* ad verba *"pendente accusatione."*

[127] C. 54, X, *de testibus et attestationibus,* II, 20.

[128] *Commentaria,* IV, 126, paragraph 6.

civil case, when testimony was furnished by persons subject to this latter condition, it was less credible than that of other people.

3) Card. Zabarella († 1417) (cited as "D. Card.") said quite simply that both *infamia facti* and *infamia iuris* impeded one from testifying in civil as well as in criminal cases.

4) Panormitanus taught that the *gravatio opinionis* was not different from the *infamia facti.*

D) Suspension and deprivation of office were sometimes in store for those who were infamous by reason of infamy of fact. For a cleric to be deprived of his office and benefice simply because of an accusation or an attack on his reputation was not the usual procedure. The glossator pointed out concerning those who were defamed that while the accusation was pending the man was to remain in his office.[129] If, however, the crime of which the cleric was suspected was of exceptional enormity and the infamy and suspicion warranted drastic action, for the effective allaying of scandal, then the bishop could deprive the cleric of his benefice as well as his office.[130]

Once the purgation was duly executed, the benefice was to be restored, except for one case. Association with a heretic if fostered knowingly and willingly called for a continuous suspension until the scandal had totally subsided, a profession of faith and an abjuration of error had been made, if that appeared necessary.[131] It is clear that the law contemplated the suspension after purgation to be of but temporary duration.[132]

Section 4. Removal of Infamy of Fact in the Decretum and in the Decretales

Infamia facti was taken away by canonical purgation, as has been shown at length. This was so because *"infamia facti"* was understood in such a restricted sense by the glossators, according

---

[129] ". . . pendente accusatione, remanet in officio suo, et interim subditi eius ei obedire tenentur. . . ."—*glossa ord. ad* c. 56, X, *de testibus et attestationibus,* II, 20, *ad verba "pendente accusatione."*

[130] C. 10, X, *de purgatione canonica,* V, 34.

[131] *Loc. cit.*

[132] Panormitanus, *Commentaria,* VII, 316.

to whom it applied to guiltless persons who had not yet sworn to their innocence in the canonical form. There were, nevertheless, several places in the law which gave evidence of the fact that the concept of *infamia facti* at times applied also to other cases, namely to persons who continued to have a bad reputation even after purgation,[133] and to persons actually guilty of that of which they had been accused.[134] In the first type of cases the removal of the bad name was effected through the performance of good works. The person concerned regained the people's respect thus: ". . .vitam suam bonis adornans operibus, ut infamia convertatur in bonam famam, et omne scandalum, et suspicio de catholicorum mentibus deleatur."[135]

The men of the time realized that in spite of a person's taking an oath of innocence some sort of suspicion could continue. Accordingly the glossator succinctly remarked: ". . . infamiam facti removere solius Dei est. . . ."[136] In such cases, however, wherein a bad reputation remained even after the purgation, infamy of fact could be easily removed through a performance of the contrary good works.[137]

In the case of infamy incurred by someone actually guilty of that of which he had been accused, public amendment was proposed as the remedy.[138]

Article VI. The Development of the Concept of *Infamia Facti* from the Time of the Medieval Writers until the Code of Canon Law

In the centuries following the *Decretum Gratiani* and the Collections of the Decretals, the writers leaned heavily on the interpretations of the earlier decretists and decretalists, on certain key laws in the *Digest* and *Code* of Justinian, and on particular laws

---

[133] C. 10, X, *de purgatione canonica,* V, 34; cf. *supra,* pp. 27-28, regarding the *gravata opinio.*

[134] C. 54, X, *de testibus et attestationibus,* II, 20.

[135] C. 10, X, *de purgatione canonica,* V, 34.

[136] *Glossa ord. ad* c. 8, X, *eod. tit., ad verbum "absolvas."*

[137] ". . . per contraria bona opera de facili tollitur infamia facti. . ."—Panormitanus, *Commentaria,* VII, 315, n. 4, on c. 8, X, *de purgatione canonica,* V, 34.

[138] C. 8, X, *de purgatione canonica,* V, 34.

in the *Decretum* and the *Decretales Gregorii IX*. The term "*infamia*" still pertained to infamy of law for the most part, though not exclusively. The association of infamy of fact with canonical purgation continued likewise in this period. Paulus Borgasius (1466-1541), writing on impediments to Holy Orders, predicated the term "*infamia*" of the bad reputation among one's neighbors which arose from an accusation of some crime and which was to be removed by way of canonical purgation.[139]

So, too, Simon Maioli (ca. 1520-1600), who also wrote on canonical impediments to Holy Orders, after listing at length different instances of the *infamia iuris,* made mention of that infamy which arises from any mortal sin, namely, canonical infamy,[140] and of the *infamia facti* or *diffamatio,* which is removed by way of proof to the contrary through canonical purgation.[141] Maioli cited Panormitanus and Sylvester Prieras (1456-1523) to substantiate his pronouncement that this *infamia facti* was of no consequence as an impediment to Orders.[142]

The term "*infamia facti,*" however, was not entirely restricted to defamation in this period of the fifteenth and sixteenth century writers. Some recognized the cases of bad reputation as adverted to in the past legislation, especially the few cases dealt with in Roman law. These cases best came under the comprehension of the expression "infamy of fact," which as a matter of fact resulted from something other than a provision of penal law. Thus, looking to the sources, Sylvester found the following to be the causes of infamy of fact:

1) any crime (to which infamy was not attached by law) ;
2) incarceration;

---

139 *Tractatus de Irregularitatibus et Impedimentis Ordinum* (Venetiis, 1574), pars VI, §23, p. 153 (hereafter cited as Borgasius).

140 Cf. *supra*, p. 17.

141 *De Irregularitatibus et Aliis Canonicis Impedimentis* (Romae, 1585), Lib. III, cap. I, p. 218 (hereafter cited as Maioli).

142 ". . . haec infamia facti nullius momenti est, quoad impedimentum, ne quis promoveatur. . . ."—*loc. cit.;* Sylvester, *Summa Silvestrina* (2 vols., Venetiis, 1601), II, p. 25, n. 7; Panormitanus, *Commentaria* V, p. 118, on c. 13, X, *de sententia et re iudicata,* II, 27.

3) having one's testimony refused because of some crime;[143]
4) derogatory words in a will;[144]
5) disciplinary correction by a judge;[145]
6) any deed considered by good and serious men as scandalous.[146]

Sylvester also looked to the sources to determine the effects of this infamy,[147] and listed the following:

1) it made one ineligible for dignities;[148]
2) it prevented one from testifying in a criminal case;[149]
3) it prevented one from making accusations;[150]
4) it prevented one from bringing an action;[151]
5) it prevented one from being advanced to Orders;[152]
6) it permitted one to contest the will of a relative who had designated an infamous person as heir;[153]
7) it occasioned the duty of canonical purgation.[154] *Infamia facti* lapsed upon proof of innocence, and could lapse also by way of dispensation at least as to its effects.[155]

Gradually, then, the authors came to consider that causes other than *diffamatio* or the accusation of having committed a crime could lead to what was termed "*infamia facti.*" Even more impor-

---

143 C. 54, X, *de testibus et attestationibus,* II, 20.
144 C. (2.11) 13, cf, *supra,* p. 7.
145 C. (2.11) 19, cf. *supra,* p. 6.
146 C. 11, C. VI, q. 1; c. 47, X, *de testibus et attestationibus,* II, 20.
147 *Summa Silvestrina,* II, p. 25, nn. 4-6.
148 Regula 87, *Liber Sextus Decretalium Bonifatii VIII.*
149 C. 54, X, *de testibus et attestationibus,* II, 20.
150 D. (48.2) 8.
151 D. (48.1) 5.
152 C. 4, X, *de accusationibus inquisitionibus et denunciationibus,* V, 1.
153 C. (3.28) 27, cf. *supra,* p. 7.
154 C. 15, X, *de accusationibus, inquisitionibus et denunciationibus,* V, 1.
155 "Potest etiam princeps disponere ut talis infamia non habeat effectum." Sylvester, *Summa Silvestrina,* II, p. 25, n. 4. In proof of this he cited Panormitanus, *Commentaria,* V, 120, n. 20, on c. 23, X, *de sententia et re iudicata,* II, 27; Panormitanus, however, in that place seemed to be dealing with infamy of law, saying that infamy when imposed by precept was also removed by way of precept.

tant than the views of these writers, however, was the practice of the Holy See, which through decisions of the Sacred Roman Rota and the Sacred Congregation of the Council indiated that *infamia facti* resulted not merely from accusations, but also by the actual commission of crimes.

The Sacred Roman Rota handled certain cases of *infamia facti* in the seventeenth century. In decisions handed down in the years 1650, 1670 and 1679, it stated that the mere accusation of a crime prevented one from acquiring a benefice only if at least a *semiplena probatio* of guilt was furnished.[156]

The Sacred Congregation of the Council, in 1661, dealt more strictly with one who was accused of homicide, declaring that the one accused should be considered as irregular in regard to promotion to Orders.[157] The author Pignatelli (1600-1675) in commenting on this decision stated:

> In reference to the promotion of a cleric to Orders there are not required conclusive proofs, but a defaming accusation producing the same effect is considered cause enough for denying him Orders; this is especially true in regard to homicide, in which case, even when there is a doubt, one should act as with a person who is irregular in view of the exceptional incompatibility of a bloody crime with an unbloody sacrifice.[158]

Since the problems of *infamia facti* usually arose in connection with Holy Orders and the conferral and administration of benefices, such cases of *infamia,* in the eighteenth century, came to be con-

---

[156] *Decisiones Rencensiores Rotae, 1558-1684* (19 vols. in 25, edd. P. Farinacius, P. Rubeus, J. B. Compagnus, Venetiis, 1618-1697, Romae, 1697-1703), pars 11, decis. 8, nn. 19, 20; pars 16, decis. 323, n. 21; pars 19, tom. 2, decis. 501 nn.. 3, 4.

[157] S. C. C., *Novarien.,* 1 oct. 1661—*Codicis Iuris Canonici Fontes,* cura Emi Petri Card. Gasparri editi (9 vols., Romae: Typis Polyglottis Vaticanis, 1923-1939. Vols. VII-IX, ed. cura et studio Emi Iustiniani Card. Serédi), n. 2769 (hereafter cited as *Fontes*).

[158] *Consultationes Canonicae* (11 vols. in 5, Coloniae Allobrogum, 1700-1711), VII, consul. 19, p. 40.

sidered by the Sacred Congregation of the Council alone. The cases belonged to this Congregation because of the extensive legislation of the Council of Trent on disciplinary matters involved in Holy Orders and benefices, and it was within the competency of the Sacred Congregation of the Council to see to the application of the provisions of the Council of Trent.[159]

This Congregation on different occasions declared that if a cleric were accused of some crime even without being condemned for it, and if he had performed penance and lived an exemplary life for a period of at least three years after the crime, he was not to be considered irregular in regard to the reception of Orders and the holding of a benefice.[160]

The Sacred Congregation decided in 1763 that if a cleric had become infamous, not because of any serious crime which he had committed, but because of numerous less serious ones, he might, after a period of penance in atonement for his former way of life, be permitted the reception of a benefice.[161]

---

159 The Fathers of the Council in the twenty-fifth session provided among other things: "Quod si in his (decretis) recipiendia aliqua difficultas oriatur, aut aliqua inciderint, quae declarationem, quod non credit, aut definitionem postulant, praeter alia remedia in hoc Concilio instituta confidit S. Synodus, beatissimum Romanum Pontificem curaturum. . . ." Pope Pius V in his *motu proprio "Alias nos"* of August 4, 1564, appointed eight cardinals to see to it that the decrees of the Council of Trent were kept; this he called the "Congregatio super executione et observantia S. Concilii Tridentini." The Congregation underwent several changes in the course of time. Its competence came to include disciplinary matters and matrimonial cases appealed to it from the Rota, except for Pauline Privilege cases, which pertained to the Holy Office.—Ojetti, *De Romana Curia* (Romae: Ex Cooperativo Typographico Manzio, 1910), pp. 81-96.

160 S. C. C., *Spoletana,* 19 ian. 1737—Fontes, n. 3467; S. C. C., *Ferrarien.,* 25 ian. 1851—*Fontes,* n. 4116.

161 S C. C., *Terulen.,* 3 iul. 1762—*Fontes,* n. 3720; 27 aug., 24 sept., 1763—*Fontes,* n. 3731.

PART II

Canonical Commentary

CHAPTER II

The Fundamental Notion of Infamy of Fact in the Code of Canon Law

Article I. The General Concept of Infamy

Two types of *infamia* are described in the Code of Canon Law: *infamia iuris* and *infamia facti.* They are distinguishable one from the other. *Infamia iuris* is a vindicative penalty, one of the twelve common vindicative penalties listed in canon 2291, and is incurred either automatically or after sentence by those who are guilty of crimes to which *infamia* is explicitly attached by the common law.[1]

Infamia facti is not a penalty in the strict canonical sense, but is rather the natural reaction of good and prudent men to the misconduct of their fellow man.[2] It is in the broad sense of the word a penalty of the natural order whereby a delinquent loses the respect of his fellows.

A delinquent may incur legal infamy and be at the same time infamous in fact once his guilt has become public. The two types of infamy, however, do not necessarily coincide. More often they do not, actually, for infamy of law is not often incurred, inasmuch as it is consequent simply upon serious crimes which are not frequently committed. One may become infamous by infamy of fact in many ways other than through the incurring of legal infamy. Then, too, one can incur automatic infamy of law occultly, and escape criticism and infamy of fact.

Infamy of fact is delineated in the Code of Canon Law more clearly than it has been delineated in any previous legislation. The term "*infamia facti*" was in the past employed by canonists and

---

[1] The crimes punishable by *infamia iuris* in the Code are listed in canons 2314, §1, 2°, 3°; 2320; 2328; 2343, §1, 2° and §2°, 2°; 2351, §1; 2357, §1; 2359, §2.

[2] Chelodi-Ciprotti, *De Delictis et Poenis,* n. 50; p. 66; Cocchi, *Commentarium,* VIII, p. 76; Regatillo, *Ius Sacramentarium* (2 vols., Sal Terrae; Santander, 1945-1946), II, p. 387.

also by the Holy See in certain decisions regarding the reception and exercise of Orders, as also the reception and retention of benefices.[3] The Code, however, presents the first legal definition, albeit a descriptive definition, of infamy of fact. In so doing, the Code has set down the way in which the term is to be understood whenever it is employed in law.

In his descriptive definition of infamy of fact, moreover, the lawgiver has seen fit to qualify somewhat the broad meaning formerly associated with this term. Before the effects of infamy of fact are dealt with, this descriptive definition of infamy of fact will be considered in detail.

Article II. The Descriptive Definition of Infamy of Fact

Canon 2293, § 3.*Infamia facti contrahitur, quando quis, ob patratum delictum vel ob pravos mores, bonam existimationem apud fideles probos et graves amisit, de quo iudicium spectat ad Ordinarium.*

Section 1. "*Infamia facti* CONTRAHITUR. . . ."

Infamy of fact may be contracted by any person, man or woman, lay, clerical or religious.[4] Infamy of fact is said to be contracted by individuals rather than imposed upon them either judicially or administratively, as is the case with punishments according to the law. Factual infamy can result, however, from a condemnation in court, be it civil or ecclesiastical, once it has become public, not because of any provision of law as such, but because of the unfavorable reaction of the people to such a condemnation and because of the crime committed.[5]

---

[3] *Supra,* pp. 32-33.

[4] Blat, *Commentarium Textum Codicis Iuris Canonici* (6 vols., Lib. II, *De Personis,* 2. ed. 1921, Lib. III, *De Rebus,* Partes II-VI, 1923, Lib. V, *De Delictis et Poenis,* 1924, Romae: Ex Typographia Pontificia in Instituto Pii X), Lib. V, p. 176 (hereafter cited as Blat).

[5] "Saepius occurrere potest ut infamia facti oriatur ex gravi condemnatione qua quis a iudice civili vel ecclesiastico mulctatus est."—Berutti, *Institutiones Iuris Canonici* (6 vols., Vol. VI, *De Delictis et Poenis,* Taurini-Romae; Marietti, 1938), p. 220 (hereafter cited as *De Delictis*).

Section 2. "Infamia facti contrahitur . . . OB PATRATUM DELICTUM. . . ."

The commission of a delict is the basic way in which infamy of fact may be incurred. There is a certain parallel here between infamy of law, which as a punishment is incurred after the commission of certain grave crimes to which the law has specifically attached this penalty, and infamy of fact, which is incurred after any crime, once all the other elements of the descriptive definition are present.

A delict as the Code envisions it may give rise to infamy of fact either directly, after the commission of a crime, or indirectly, after the observance of the penalty which is consequent upon the commission of a crime. These causes of infamy will be more easily understood under the separate titles of: a), the commission of a delict, and b), the observance of a penalty.

A. The Commission of a Delict

"Delict" is precisely defined in the Code as an external and morally imputable violation of the law to which there is added a canonical sanction, at least an indeterminate one.[6] Three elements are contained in that definition: a), moral imputability; b), an external fact; and c), a legal sanction. If the *delictum* in the descriptive definition of *infamia facti* is to be understood in a strict sense, then all three of these essential elements of the canonical delict must be present in a misdeed before there can be what is termed infamy of fact. There seems to be no intrinsic reason for assuming that there is present here any exception to the general understanding of *"delictum"* as it is defined in the Code.

This provision of the present law, (namely the provision whereby there is postulated for the contracting of infamy of fact some misdeed so serious that it qualifies also as a delict, as the Code understands "delict"), is one of the ways in which the Code has modified the former and broader understanding of *infamia facti.* Thus Gasparri (1852-1934)[7] and Maupied (1814-1878)[8] spoke in

---

[6] Canon 2197, §1.

[7] *De Sacra Ordinatione,* I, 196.

[8] *Juris Canonici Universi Compendium* (2 vols., accurante J. Migne, Parisiis: Ex Typis L. Migne, 1861-1863), II, col. 1032.

a more generic way of a sin or base deed as being the basis for and the cause of infamy of fact. Sinfulness is even yet the basis for factual infamy, since all delicts are sins, and a depraved way of life (*pravi mores*) indicates a seriously sinful way of life. If one prescind, however, from this depraved way of life, the individual acts which lead to infamy of fact as the Code describes it are *delicts,* and not *sins* understood generically.

It may happen that a person will be accused of a crime of which he is innocent, and in consequence of the accusation will lose his good reputation among good and prudent Catholics. Is such a person infamous by infamy of fact? In strict parlance he is not infamous, since he has not committed the crime of which he has been accused, and the Code demands for infamy of fact that it be the effect of a *perpetrated* crime. The presumption is that good and prudent Catholics will not think another blameworthy on the basis of a simple accusation. The bad reputation which results from an accusation is something less than the Code envisions in its descriptive definition of infamy of fact. Infamy of fact results from a perpetrated delict, and not from the accusation thereof. This is an innovation in the notion of infamy of fact. Formerly *infamia facti* was identified with the loss of reputation which resulted from the accusation of having committed a crime.[9] This was pointed out by the glossators in their glosses on Roman law,[10] on the *Decretum Gratiani,*[11] and on the *Decretales Gregorii IX.*[12]

In the event, however, that strong proofs and indications can and do accompany the accusation, it is logical that prudent people will believe that the one accused is guilty of some crime. For all practical purposes, then, the individual accused becomes infamous by infamy of fact, since he will be made to observe the effects of infamy. The people and the ordinary, who ultimately judges as to

---

[9] *Supra,* pp. 21-22.

[10] C. (2.13) 6; D. (48.1) 5.

[11] C. 39, C. II, q. 7; c. 8, C. III, q. 5.

[12] Cc. 1, 4, X, *de accusationibus, inquisitionibus et denunciationibus,* V, 1; cc. 1-15, X, *de purgatione canonica,* V, 34; c. 56, X, *de testibus et attestationibus,* II, 20, *passim.*

the presence of *infamia facti*, can only judge on the external facts as they are presented for their judgment. Though the unfortunate individual does not deserve the stigma of infamy of fact, he has incurred factual infamy in an improper sense of the word, since he has not been guilty of a *delictum patratum*, but is merely thought to be guilty of a delict. When authors say, therefore, that innocent people can incur infamy of fact, it is in this improper sense of the word that infamy is to be understood.[13]

Once a person has been proved innocent of an accusation, he is no longer to be considered infamous. The judgment as to whether or not there is present any infamy of fact according to the Code's definition pertains to the ordinary.[14] If the ordinary judges that a person is innocent of the crime of which he has been accused, he at the same time judges that *infamia facti* is not present, and that the individual is no longer bound by the effects of infamy of fact. When, therefore, it becomes clear, either with or without the judgment of the ordinary, that an individual is innocent of some charge, he in no way is to be said to be infamous by infamy of fact.

If a certain bad opinion concerning the person once accused and later cleared of any guilt persists beyond the time when his innocence is made known, this bad opinion is not infamy of fact, nor is the individual in question bound by the restrictions consequent upon *infamia facti*, e.g., he would not be impeded from Holy Orders. Before setting aside the canonical effects of infamy of fact, however, the ordinary might require a short period of time

---

[13] "It can happen that an innocent person may be affected with infamy of fact. Among upright and serious-minded Catholics the innocent person has been judged to be guilty, and unless their judgment is proved to be erroneous, the subjectively innocent person still incurs factual infamy."—Vogelpohl, *The Simple Impediments to Holy Orders*, The Catholic University of America Canon Law Studies, n. 224 (Washington, D. C.: The Catholic University of America Press, 1945), p. 153 (hereafter cited as Vogelpohl); Regatillo, *Ius Sacramentarium*, II, 86; Cappello, *Tractatus Canonicus de Sacramentis* (5 vols., Vols. I, II, V, 5. ed., 1947, Vols. III, IV, 2. ed., 1942, 1947, Romae: Marietti), IV, n. 525, p. 391 (hereafter cited *De Sacramentis*); Merkelbach, *Summa Theologiae Moralis* (8. ed., 3 vols., Montréal: Typis Desclée de Brouwer, 1947), III, n. 745.

[14] ". . . de quo iudicium spectat ad Ordinarium."—*infra*, pp. 65-68.

to elapse until even this slight loss of respect should be overcome, for the sake of preventing scandal.[15]

In summary it may be said, then, that since the law requires a perpetrated delict for infamy of fact, it will seldom happen that accusations will cause infamy of fact even in the improper sense of the word. When, however, accusations do cause an infamy improperly so called, the infamy continues only as long as the one accused is held guilty, and ceases when his innocence is made known.[16]

Since moral culpability is postulated for a delict properly so called,[17] and a perpetrated delict, in turn, is the basis for infamy of fact, the question arises as to whether infamy of fact is present when an external violation of the law has been committed without malice or culpability on the part of the individual who objectively is to be regarded as having committed a crime.[18] This situation is parallel to that wherein an innocent person is accused of a crime. Practically the individual is to be considered infamous by infamy of fact, though strictly he has not become infamous by reason of infamy of fact, for it arises from a perpetrated delict. When it is said that subjective culpability and malice are not essential to the existence of *infamia facti,*[19] it is in this practical applied sense that

[15] The problem as to whether or not the *gravata opinio* which continued to exist after a person had been cleared of guilt was *infamia facti* was, even to the medieval writers, a matter of controversy. The majority of the writers, including Hostiensis and Ioannes Andreae, thought that *gravata opinio* and *infamia facti* were not the same, whereas Panormitanus thought that they were the same.—*supra,* pp. 27-28.

[16] "Accidere potest aliquando, ut infamia facti laborent etiam innocentes, si ut rei habeantur: qui idcirco arceantur ab ordinibus suscipiendis *donec eorum innocentia cognita fuerit.*"—Cappello, *De Sacramentis,* IV, n. 525, p. 391.

[17] "Nomine delicti, iure ecclesiastico, intelligitur externa et *moraliter imputabilis* legis violatio. . . ."—canon 2195, §1.

[18] The character of a moral act which makes it attributable to a certain person is called its imputability. The imputability of a crime depends on the malice (*dolus*) of the culprit, which is the deliberate will to violate the law, or on his culpability (*culpa*), which may be either culpable ignorance of the law or failure to use due diligence.—canons 2199; 2200, §1.

[19] Vogelpohl, p. 152.

such a statement is to be understood. Even in abstraction from subjective culpability, if all the other elements of a delict and infamy of fact are present, then, in the eyes of the law, the person involved is infamous, and is bound by the effects of infamy of fact. There is a presumption of law that, when a person violates the law, he does so with malice (i.e., with a deliberate will to violate the law), which presumption persists until innocence is proved.[20] Proof of innocence is at the same time an indication that infamy of fact does not exist.

Proof of innocence in the case of those who were falsely accused should evoke from the good and serious-minded people, whom canon 2293, § 3, contemplates, an admission of their misjudgment, and the reinstatement of the one who had previously been thought guilty of some crime into his former status.

Canon 2195 also requires as essential to the definition of a crime that at least an indetermine sanction be attached to the perpetrated violation of the law.[21] An indetermine sanction is placed on every violation of the law by canon 2222, § 1, which canon permits a superior to punish transgressions regardless of whether or not a penalty was otherwise provided by law or precept, if the act gave rise to scandal or was of a special gravity.[22] The provision of canon 2222 brings any such violations within the definition of a crime as stated in canon 2195. Any violation such as causes loss of reputation will certainly be one which causes scandal or which is of a special gravity. A violation of a law which causes scandal or which is of a special gravity is a delict strictly so called because of the indetermine sanction placed on

---

[20] Canon 2200, § 2.

[21] "Nomine delicti, iure ecclesiastico, intelligitur externa et moraliter imputabilis legis violatio cui addita sit *sanctio canonica saltem indeterminata.*"—canon 2195, § 1.

[22] ". . . canon 2222, § 1, principium generale seu legem generalem statuit qua omnis ordinis ecclesiastici perturbatio poena indeterminata punitur, quo fit ut illo canone lex generalis poenalis praevia contra quamlibet iuris socialis ecclesiastici violationem habeatur et elementum legale modo generali statuitur pro omnibus casibus in quibus elementa delicti formalia seu dolus una cum perturbatione ordinis socialis inveniuntur."—Coronata, *Institutiones Iuris Canonici* (2. ed., 5 vols., Taurini, Romae: Marietti, 1939-1947), IV, 4 (hereafter cited *Institutiones*).

such a violation, as long as all the other conditions of canon 2222 are verified. Thus the loss of reputation consequent upon such a delict is infamy of fact in the proper sense of canon 2293, § 3. It always remains for the ordinary, however, to decide whether or not infamy is present in any given case, even infamy of fact in the less strict sense of the word, as it has been described.[23]

B. The Observance of a Penalty

The perpetration of a delict can bring on infamy of fact only after it has become public, as is obvious. An occult crime, either materially, as to its commission, or formally, as to the culprit, does not induce infamy of fact. One of the ways in which the commission of a delict as also culpability for its commission becomes public is through the observance of the penalty. The Code recognizes this fact by naming anticipated infamy (*periculum infamiae*) as a more urgent case which excuses one from observing a penalty,[24] and which gives the confessor reason to release a penitent from the obligation of observing a vindicative penalty,[25] to absolve a penitent from a censure,[26] and to dispense a penitent from an irregularity.[27] The law by such provisions demonstrates the greater good involved in the maintaining of a good reputation than in the external observance of a penalty or an impediment.

It is infamy of fact and not infamy of law which is signified by the *periculum* in the canons cited above. A consideration of the penal laws shows why this is so. Infamy in these matters is treated as a consequence of a penalty. Now, the observance of a penalty is a good act, by which a penal law is brought into execution, and infamy of law is a real penalty. Since a good act cannot be accompanied with a penalty, it need never be feared that the danger of infamy of law will attend the observance of a penalty.[28]

---

[23] *Supra*, pp. 40-41.

[24] Canon 2232, § 1.

[25] Canon 2290, § 1.

[26] Canon 2254, § 1.

[27] Canon 990, § 2.

[28] Kurczynski, *De Natura et Observantia Poenarum Latae Sententiae*, Katolicki Univwersytet Lubelski Rozprawy Doktorski, tom. 8 (Lublin, Towarzystwo Naukowe Katolickiego Uniwersytetu Lubelskiego, 1938), p. 108 (hereafter cited as Kurczynski).

One may ask just how the danger of becoming infamous by infamy of fact excuses one from the observance of penalties and irregularities, and also how this danger furnishes a reason for the extraordinary absolution from censures. A brief consideration of the canons on these matters will help in the answering of these questions.

First of all, it must be pointed out that every ecclesiastical law involves a certain moral obligation.[29] This obligation when pertaining to penal laws as such is an obligation for those who have broken the law to observe the penalty which is consequent upon the commission of a crime. The binding effect of ecclesiastical penalties is deduced from the provision of canon 2232, § 1: "Poena latae sententiae, sive medicinalis sive vindicativa, delinquentem, qui delicti sibi sit conscius, ipso facto in utroque foro tenent. . . ."

Certain causes, however, are said to excuse one from the observance of automatic penalties, or to warrant absolution from such penalties.[30] As for the observance of penalties, the only excusing

---

[29] St. Thomas, *Summa Theologica*, I^{a}, II^{ae}, q. XC, art. IV, 2.

[30] These causes may be divided *ex parte intellectus,* and *ex parte voluntatis,* according to this schema:

- *I. ex parte intellectus*
  - psycho-physical causes, e.g., impuberty and insanity.
  - ideological causes, e.g., doubt and ignorance.
- *II. ex parte voluntatis*
  - absolute causes
    - physical, e.g., external force and constraint.
    - spiritual, e.g., the necessity of violating a superior law in the observance of a penalty.
  - moral causes
    - physical, e.g., harm to health or fortune.
    - spiritual, e.g., scandal and infamy of fact.

Cf. Kurczynski, pp. 99-103.

cause mentioned in the Code is the danger of infamy or of scandal in canons 2232, § 1, and 2290, § 1. The other causes are treated according to the general norms of canons 15 and 16.

The excusing of one from the observance of a penalty according to canons 2232, § 1, and 2290, § 1, does not however mean that the penalty is totally removed; it means simply that the penalty is suspended in such a way that a delinquent is for a certain period of time free from the obligation of acting as if bound by a penalty.

Canon 2232, § 1, states that ". . . ante sententiam tamen declaratoriam a poena observanda delinquens excusatur quoties eam servare sine infamia nequit. . . ." This refers to vindicative penalties as well as to censures.

Canon 2290, § 1, grants to confessors the power to dispense penitents from the observance of vindicative penalties when there is danger of infamy or the threat of scandal if the penalty were observed.[31] The canon provides not for a *dispensation* from vindicative penalties, except when recourse is impossible as stated in the second paragraph,[32] but for a *suspension of the observance* of vindicative penalties.

Since canon 2232, § 1, excuses a delinquent from the observance of a penalty if he cannot observe it without infamy, it may be asked what is gained by the faculty conceded to the confessor of suspending the observance of a penalty in a particular case. The use of this faculty as granted in canon 2290, it is answered, excuses the delinquent in an absolute way, so that even if it happens that there is no longer any danger that infamy will arise from the observance of the penalty, the delinquent still does not have to

---

[31] "In casibus occultis urgentioribus, si ex observatione poenae vindicativae latae sententiae, reus seipsum proderet cum infamia et scandalo, quilibet confessarius potest in foro sacramentali obligationem servandae poenae suspendere iniuncto onere recurrendi saltem intra mensem per epistolam et per confessarium, si id fieri possit sine gravi incommodo, reticito nomine, ad S. Poenitentiariam vel ad Episcopum facultate praeditum et standi eius mandatis."—canon 2290, § 1.

[32] "Et si in aliquo casu extraordinario hic recursus sit impossibilis, tunc ipsemet confessarius potest dispensationem concedere ad normam canon 2254, § 3."—canon 2290, § 2.

observe the penalty until the reply from the superior arrives. This is a greater benefit than that provided in canon 2232, § 1, whereby the delinquent is free from the observance of the penalty only as long as the observance would jeopardize his reputation.[33] Moreover, canon 2232, § 1, sets up an excuse in the external forum only with reference to such acts as occasion infamy, while canon 2290, § 1, makes it possible that a complete suspension of the vindicative penalty be granted.[34]

As for the absolution from penalties (which absolution pertains only to the medicinal penalties known as censures), canon 2254, § 1, mentions two moral-spiritual causes which warrant this absolution, namely the danger of serious scandal or infamy, and the hardship for a delinquent to remain for a long time in the state of mortal sin. This absolution means, of course, that the penalty is taken away.

The more urgent case as it has reference to dispensation from irregularities is contained in canon 990, § 2. Under this law any simple confessor can dispense from all irregularities arising from an occult delict, except the cases of voluntary homicide and abortion, provided that there is an urgent necessity for the dispensation, namely the impossibility of approaching the ordinary without danger of grave harm or infamy. This power is restricted to enabling the penitent to exercise licitly the Orders which he has already received, but is not extended to enabling the penitent to be promoted to further Orders.

The Regular confessor, however, in virtue of papal privileges, can dispense so as to enable such an advancement to Sacred Orders, and, moreover, there is no need for these confessors to

---

[33] Coronata, *Institutiones,* IV, 264; Vermeersch-Creusen, *Epitome Iuris Canonici* (3 vols., Vol. I, 6. ed., 1937, Vol. II, 5. ed., 1934, Vol. III, 5. ed., Bruxellis: Dessain, 1936), III n. 491 (hereafter cited as *Epitome*); Woywod, *A Practical Commentary on the Code of Canon Law* (4 ed., 2 vols., New York: Wagner, 1929), II, p. 502 (hereafter cited as *A Practical Commentary*).

[34] J. J. Christ, *Dispensation from Vindicative Penalties,* The Catholic University of America Canon Law Studies, n. 174 (Washington, D. C.: The Catholic University of America Press, 1943), p. 179 (hereafter cited as Christ).

determine whether or not there is present any urgent necessity.[35]

When actually can there be said to be a danger of infamy if a penalty or irregularity is observed? First of all, the penalty or irregularity must be occult in the sense of canon 2297, 4°, i.e., not public. A crime or irregularity may be occult *absolutely,* i.e. everywhere, or *relatively,* i.e. only in certain places. In whichever way a crime or irregularity is occult, the danger of infamy may be present.

A crime may also be said to be occult *materially,* if the very performance of the delictual act is as yet unknown, or *formally,* if the imputability of the crime is unknown, i.e. it is not known that the one who committed the criminal act did so with malice and culpability.[36] When a crime is materially occult, it is beyond question that the culprit may still have his good reputation, and that by observing the penalty he would make known his guilt and thus would become infamous. If the crime is formally occult, however, and the people who know the culprit who performed the act do at the same time *positively* excuse him from any blame, (e.g., on the grounds that the crime was performed by him in perfect drunkenness or passion), then certainly the danger of infamy will arise from the observance of the penalty. The fact that people already think ill of the person in question does not weaken the force of this statement, for it is only when people realize that the person is fully responsible for a crime that they will lose all respect for him to the degree that infamy can be said to be present.

When the people do not positively excuse the culprit from blame, but have *doubts* whether or not he performed the crime with perfect knowledge and free consent of the will, then it is probably right to think that even in such a case there is verified the danger that infamy will arise from the observance of the penalty. The reason for thinking this is that, since the delinquent

[35] Shuhler, *Privileges of Regulars to Absolve and Dispense,* The Catholic University of America Canon Law Studies, n. 186 (Washington, D. C.: The Catholic University of America Press, 1943), p. 163; Schaefer, *De Religiosis* (3. ed., Romae: Typis Polyglottis Vaticanis, 1940), pp. 830-831.

[36] Canons 2197, 4°; 2199. It is true that, as far as the law is concerned, when an external violation of the law has been committed, malice is presumed in the external forum until the contrary is proved.—canon 2200,

has not definitely lost his good name as yet, he will, by observing the penalty, dispel all doubts as to his guilt.[37]

In the cases envisioned in canon 2232, § 1, the delinquent himself must decide how great a danger there is that infamy will result from the observance of the penalty connected with the crime which he committed. This same obligation belongs to the confessor in the cases of absolution from censures and of dispensations from irregularities and from the observance of vindicative penalties. The confessor, however, may rely, and at times he must rely, on the word of the penitent as to the probability of infamy, as in the case of suspension from office for a particular time, or of a refusal to accept a particular benefice offered to him.[38]

The danger of infamy will more surely be present in the observance of certain kinds of penalties than in the observance of others. Thus in *latae sententiae* penalties which deprive one of a benefice,[39] of the fruits of a benefice,[40] of ecclesiastical pensions,[41] or of the episcopacy,[42] there will ordinarily be a danger of infamy in the observance of the penalty attached to a crime which is still occult. Other penalties which deprive the culprit of certain rights are not so apt to cause infamy through the observance of these privitive penalties, since the exercise of the rights in question might be foregone for some reason other than because of the observance of the penalties, e.g., because of illness or simple neglect. Such penal privations include the privation of the right of patronage,[43]

§ 2. In the matter here considered, however, the *opinion* of those who know of the violation of the law is of greater importance than this presumption of law. The opinion of these people may be one whereby they, for some reason, excuse from guilt the one who violated the law; thus, for example, they may excuse him because they believe that he performed the evil act in such a fit of passion that he could not have performed a free act of the intellect and the will, even though that reason may not be rooted in the truth.

[37] Kurczynski, p. 110.

[38] Christ, p. 181.

[39] Canons 2266; 2336, § 1; 2346, 2343, § 1, 1°.

[40] Canons 2381, 1°; 2266; 1475, § 2.

[41] Canon 2266.

[42] Canon 2398.

[43] Canons 2346; 2393; 2392, 2°; 2394, 3°, and any canons which deprive

of the episcopacy before having taken possession of the see, or of the right of active or passive voice in ecclesiastical elections.[44] It may happen, too, that suspensions, e.g., suspensions from the celebration of Mass,[45] from the hearing of confessions,[46] from the exercise of the power of Orders,[47] from the performance of acts of jurisdiction,[48] etc., can be observed without any danger of infamy. If, however, there is any danger of infamy, then, of course, there is a reason for the non-observance of the penalty.

Is there danger that infamy will result from the observance of invalidating penalties, i.e., of penalties which render invalid the acts which the delinquent performs in violation of the penalty he incurred?[49] It is the common teaching of canonists that these penalties *can* be observed without the danger of infamy.[50] The reason for this view has its basis in the very nature of the invalidating penalty itself, which as a moral and not a physical privation has its whole force because of the law itself, in such a way that it merely obliges the delinquents to *abstain* from performing certain acts which legally they are not capable of performing. A negative attitude generally does not in itself indicate that a person is not performing certain acts *because of a penalty*.[51] It may possibly happen in certain exceptional cases, as Kurczynski suggests, that

culprits of the exercise of authorized ecclesiastical acts, since the right of patronage is one of these authorized acts. Cf. canon 2256, 2°.

44 Canons 2368, § 1; 2394, 3°; 2265, § 1, 1°; 2391, § 1; 2392, 2°; 2393.

45 Canon 2410.

46 Canons 2366, 2368, § 1.

47 Canons 2400; 2372; 2387; 2374.

48 Canons 2402; 2386; 2375; 2265, § 1, 1°.

49 Invalidating penalties, *poenae inhabilitantes,* are listed in canons 2390, § 2; 2394, 1°; 2395. Cf. also canons 2298, 5°; 2291, § 2. *Infamia iuris* is a *poena inhabilitans;* cf. canon 2294, § 1, and *supra,* p. 37, note 1.

50 Salucci, *Il Diritto Penale secondo il Codice di Diritto Canonico* (2 vols., Subiaco: Tipografia dei Monasteri, 1926-1930), I, p. 152, 3°; Sole, *Praelectiones in Lib. V Codicis Iuris Canonici, De Delictis et Poenis* (Romae; Pustet, 1920), n. 127 (hereafter cited *De Delictis*); Claeys Bouuaert-Simenon, *Manuale Juris Canonici* (3 vols., Vol. I, 5. ed., 1939; Vol. III, 5. ed., 1943, Gandae et Leodii: Seminarium Gandavense et Leodense), III, n. 528 (hereafter cited as Claeys Bouuert-Simenon); Cocchi, *Commentarium,* VIII, n. 46.

51 Kurczynski, p. 120.

infamy may also arise in consequence of the observance of invalidating penalties. A priest, for instance, who has often made known to his ordinary that he would like to be assigned a certain benefice, and who unquestionably has all the qualities necessary for being given such a benefice, would not be obliged to make known a crime he may have committed and the invalidating penalty which he had incurred, if the ordinary commanded the priest to accept the benefice.[52] In such a case the priest could accept the benefice, and thereby disregard the observance of the invalidating penalty. For convalidating his title to the benefice, the beneficiary should have recourse to the Sacred Penitentiary.[53]

This case is one which pertains to canon 2232, § 1, wherein the delinquent himself must determine the extent of the danger of infamy. It is, as has been said, the confessor's obligation to determine this danger in such cases as may be presented to him in the confessional, and as are envisioned in canon 990, § 2; 2254 § 1; and 2290, § 1. When in these cases the confessor has at least a positive and probable reason for judging that there is present the danger of infamy if the irregularity or penalty were observed, even though he has some doubt in this regard, he can by virtue of canon 209 validly and licitly dispense or absolve according to the need that exists.[54] Even if it becomes evident subsequently that there was actually no danger of infamy at the time of the confession, although the doubt concerning its presence had arisen from a prudent judgment, the suspension of the penalty or the dispensation from the censure or the irregularity is certainly valid, if the other provisions of canons 990, 2254, and 2290 were duly observed.[55]

Section 3. *"Infamia facti contrahitur* . . . OB PRAVOS MORES. . . ."

The second way in which one becomes infamous by infamy of fact is through corrupt morals. It is distinguished from the first way indicated in the law in that the *delictum patratum* looks to

[52] *Ibid.*, p. 121.
[53] *Ibid.*, p. 122.
[54] Christ, p. 181.
[55] Christ, pp. 181-182.

some single evil act, while the expression *pravi mores* denotes a habitual waywardness. The occasional failures of a sinner will not ordinarily produce loss of reputation among the faithful. Certainly the presumption must be that they will not, since the weakness of man, and the possibility of consequent penitence on his part, and the supreme mercy of Almighty God are objects of our faith. The sinners who become infamous, however, are those who repeatedly and openly commit serious sin or who remain in the near occasion of serious sin, and who make no noticeable amendment and are, therefore, observed to be impenitent. Even the occasional appearance at the confessional does not rule out infamy for recidivous sinners, those namely who repeatedly fall back into the same sins after many confessions without any amendment.[56]

The Code uses so strong an expression as *"pravi mores"* in order that we may realize what serious evil a man must do before he will lose his standing in society. It will not be difficult, ordinarily, to determine whether or not a man has lost his good name, but when there is a doubt whether he is infamous to the point of being deprived of certain ecclesiastical rights and privileges, then the solution of the doubt may be found in the terms of the descriptive definition of canon 2293.

Sinners who because of corrupt morals become infamous, it is clear, are those who are guilty of sins that are public, serious, and numerous or continuous, i.e., habitual. But just as there is a greater degree of evil in a delinquent than in a sinner, so also those who have corrupt morals may be considered as people who lead more seriously sinful lives than the "public sinners" of which the Code makes mention.[57] *"Publici peccatores"* has a more generic meaning than has *"infames ob pravos mores,"* that is to say, among the public sinners are to be included those who are infamous by infamy of fact.[58] The converse of this does not necessarily hold true. Although the commission of a grave sin which is publicly known and which is still unrepented suffices for the notion of a

---

[56] Cappello, *De Sacramentis,* II, 548.

[57] Cf. canons 693, § 1; 1066; 1240, § 1, 6°.

[58] Cf. canon 855, § 1.

public sinner,[59] it does not seem to suffice for the notion of a person infamous because of corrupt morals.

Coronata by way of exception demands for the essential notion of public sinners that they publicly and notoriously live habitually in the state of sin. He emphasizes the necessity of the continuance or perseverance in such a sinful state if there is to be question of a *peccator publicus*.[60] This particular understanding of the public sinner is, for all practical purposes, the same as that which should be predicated of the person infamous by infamy of fact because of corrupt morals.

It is said that the sins which lead to infamy of fact must be serious and numerous, or continuous, as for example in the case of those who live in concubinage. The sins must also be public. The extent and the nature of this publicity is to be considered under the section dealing with the people among whom the infamy exists.[61]

Infamy of fact arising from "*pravi mores*" is an extremely relative thing by reason of such elements as the locale, the time and the person involved. As regards place, for instance, different countries have different standards of modesty, different degrees of sensitivity to certain sins, and different degrees of repugnance to certain crimes. Regatillo suggests as an instance of this that in certain places habitual blasphemers would be considered infamous; in other places they would not be judged so harshly.[62]

The causes of infamy vary from age to age. Before the Code many occupations were considered so base as to bring about infamy on the part of the one so employed. Such were the positions held by tavern-keepers, executioners, actors, musicians and

---

[59] Cappello, *De Sacramentis,* I, 56; Augustine, *A Commentary on the New Code of Canon Law* (8 vols., St. Louis Book Co., Vol. IV, 3 ed., 1925, Vol. VIII, 3. ed., 1931), IV, 230 (hereafter cited as Augustine); Heneghan, *The Marriages of Unworthy Catholics: Canons 1065 and 1066,* The Catholic University of America Canon Law Studies, n. 188 (Washington, D. C.: The Catholic University of America Press, 1944), p. 113.

[60] *Institutiones,* I, p. 914, especially note 9.

[61] *Infra,* pp. 60-65.

[62] *Ius Sacramentarium,* I, 42.

policemen.[63] These occupations at the present time do not, as such, lead to infamy of fact. On the other hand, membership in the Communist party today would certainly bring on infamy, whereas two decades ago the same reaction would not necessarily have been had.

Finally, many offenses, even slight ones, could cause a person of high estate to lose his reputation. The same offenses would not produce the same effect if they had been committed by one of lesser estate.[64] Gasparri pointed out, for example, that drunkenness in a priest would cause him to lose his good reputation, whereas it would make a layman unworthy of the clerical state, but not necessarily infamous.[65]

What is the relation between infamy and scandal? The acts of those who are infamous may at the same time cause scandal, but infamy is not the same as scandal. The danger of scandal is the reason, actually, for preventing those who are infamous from receiving an ecclesiastical position and exercising its functions. Scandal, according to St. Thomas, is a ". . . *dictum vel factum minus rectum praebens alteri occasionem ruinae spiritualis.*" There is usually a division of scandal into active and passive scandal, active scandal being applied to the action itself which offers the occasion of sinning, and passive scandal to the sin which may follow from the occasion offered. A scandalous action presents the occasion of sin to one's fellow man; an infamous action causes one to lose his own good reputation among his fellow men. When the law accordingly mentions the danger of scandal or of infamy as the two urgent considerations which warrant the non-observance of a penalty, or the dispensation from a penalty or an irregularity,[67] it is the *common good* with which it is concerned

[63] Vogelpohl, pp. 151-152; Prümmer, *Manuale Iuris Canonici* (Friburgi Brisgoviae: Herder & Co., 1927), p. 667; Sipos, *Enchiridion Iuris Canonici* (Pécs: Typographia "Haladás R. T.", 1926), p. 942 (hereafter cited as *Enchiridion*).

[64] P. Gasparri, *De Sacra Ordinatione,* I, 199.

[65] *Loc. cit.*

[66] *Summa Theologica,* IIª IIªᵉ, q. XLIII, a. I.

[67] Canons 990, § 1; 2232, § 1; 2254, § 1; 2290, § 1; 2367, § 1; *supra,* pp. 44-51.

when it mentions scandal, and one's *personal good* when it makes mention of infamy.[68]

Section 4. "Infamia facti contrahitur, quando quis. . . . BONAM EXISTIMATIONEM . . . AMISIT. . . ."

The good esteem of others is what is signified by *existitmatio;* this is what is lost or injured through crime or a sinful way of life. The supreme personal right one has to a good reputation has always been the object of the Church's concern. Reputation (*existimatio* or *fama*) is the common estimate of the qualities of some person as he or she is discussed.[69] The right to this good reputation is a matter of justice. There is even said to be a right to a good reputation which is had undeservedly, which right is rooted in the fact that great harm to the common good would arise if it were permissible to speak openly of the occult defects of others.[70]

Authors dealing with Roman law sometimes link the word "*existimatio,*" as used in our law today, with the Romans' concept of personality, the *caput.* The *caput* was the juristic personality of the individual and was composed of three elements: 1) freedom; 2) citizenship; and 3) family status. Sometimes a fourth is added—*existimatio* or civic honor.[71] The Romans' civic honor signified full qualification in the eyes of the law. Loss of honor, also in the legal sense, signified partial disqualification in the eyes of the law.

If a man was deprived of the three constituent parts of *caput,* namely liberty, citizenship and family status, he was legally dead, no longer a subject of rights. Such a complete forfeiture (*capitis diminutio maxima*) reduced him to slavery; but a partial forfeiture of rights through his loss of citizenship and family status let him

---

[68] "*Ratio vitandi scandali directe bono publico, ratio vitandae infamiae directe bono privato prospicit.*"—Coronata, *Institutiones,* IV, 187-188.

[69] "Fama est communis aestimatio de alicuius perfectionibus sermone prolata."—Noldin-Schmitt, *Summa Theologiae Moralis* (3 vols., Oeniponte-Lipsiae: Sumptibus et Typis Feliciani Rauch, Vol. II, 27. ed., 1941, Vol. III, 26. ed., 1940), II, 584 (hereafter cited as Noldin-Schmitt).

[70] Noldin-Schmitt, II, 585.

[71] Bernard-Sherman, n. 341, p. 104; Sohm, p. 182.

retain his liberty (*capitis diminutio media*), as for example when a man was banished permanently.[72]

Sometimes the civic personality was not lost, but it sustained some detriment in a lesser degree, as when the individual's reputation was impaired. This *minutio existimationis* may be defined as the impairment of a man's civic honor without producing *capitis diminutio*. In other words, without destroying his previous personality, it operated merely to diminish his personal qualifications in the eyes of the law.[73]

The *minutio existimationis,* was effected at various periods by the censor, by the praetor and by the judges, developed into the *infamia iuris,* by reason of Gaius' declaration that all who were placed under disabilities by the praetorian edict were thenceforth infamous,[74] and also into *infamia facti,* by reason of the provisions of the law concerning the *"turpes."*[75]

The canonical *infamia facti* is not to be identified simply with a total loss of honor because of the use of the word *"amisit,"* for it may also connote but a partial loss of honor, just as was provided in the concept of *minutio existimationis* as opposed to *capitis diminutio maxima* in the Roman law.[76]

The expressions *bona existimatio* and *bona fama* are both used in the Code of Canon Law.[77] *Bona fama* and *bona existimatio* both signify a good reputation, and no one denies that they are equivalent terms.[78] Logically the negatives of these expressions, *amissio bonae existimationis* (in canons 2147, § 2, 3°, and 2293, § 3) and

[72] Sohm, p. 183.

[73] D. (50.13) 5; cf. Sohm, p. 183.

[74] *Supra,* p. 4.

[57] *Supra,* p. 5.

[76] "Infamia . . . est non amissio existimationis . . . sed diminutio existimationis. . . ." D'Angelo, I (pars I), p. 278; ". . . infamia est amissio vel deminutio . . existimationis. . . ."—Beste, *Introductio in Codicem* (3. ed., Collegeville, Minnesota: St. John's Abbey Press, 1946), p. 950 in canon 2293, § 1 (hereafter cited as Beste).

[77] These two expressions occur in canons 2147, § 2, 3°; the expression *bona fama* occurs also in canons 2355; 1975, § 1; 1657, § 1.

[78] Cf. Beste, p. 950; Blat., Lib. V, p. 176.

infamia facti (in canon 2293, § 3) should also be equivalent. Sole († 1928)[79] and Coronata[80] indicate that this is so.

Noval (1861-1838)[81] and Connor,[82] however, distinguish between loss of esteem and infamy of fact as mentioned in canon 2293, § 3. Infamy of fact, they point out, always entails a loss of esteem; canon 2293, § 3, states this. Loss of esteem, on the other hand. does not always entail infamy of fact. This difference derives from the various elements that give rise to infamy of fact and simple loss of esteem. Infamy of fact connotes a loss of esteem which arises from the commission of a crime or from corrupt morals. Simple loss of esteem may arise from causes other than these. The phrases *"ob patratum delictum"* and *"ob pravos mores"* qualify the expresssion *"amissio bonae existimationis"* in the Code's description of *infamia facti*, and therefore limit the scope of the meaning of loss of estem in this description. Infamy of fact is, then, more specific than loss of esteem, by reason simply of the more limited ways in which infamy of fact is caused.

When in the Code it is stated that one of the causes for the removal of an irremovable pastor is the *"bonae existimationis amissio penes probos et graves viros,"*[83] it is not necessarily infamy of fact which is signified. The canon to which reference is made lists the way sin which the loss of reputation may come about, namely through levity in the pastor's way of life, through the recent detection of a crime committed at some time in the past, and through the loss of reputation on the part of the members of the pastor's household or of relatives who live with him, unless through their dismissal the good reputation of the pastor can be

79 "Iamvero fama, absolute dicta, est bona hominum existimatio; hinc infamia est privatio huius existimationis, seu est mala hominum existimatio."—Sole, *De Delictis*, p. 194.

80 "Codex noster de infamia canonica loquitur seu de amissione bonae famae canonicae."—*Institutiones*, IV, 267.

81 *Commentarium Codicis Iuris Canonici, De Processibus* (2 vols., Romae, 1920-1932), II, 481 (hereafter cited as Noval).

82 *The Administrative Removal of Pastors*, The Catholic University of America Canon Law Studies, n. 104 (Wa.hington, D. C.: The Catholic University of America, 1937), p. 37.

83 Canon 2147, § 2, 3°.

restored. The second of these ways in which the loss of reputation may come about as it is described in canon 2147, § 2, 3°, namely, through the detection of a crime committed at some time in the past, would, so it seems, qualify as a loss of reputation *ob delictum,* and, with all the other elements of canon 2293, § 3, present, would result in infamy of fact. The other two causes for loss of reputation mentioned in canon 2147, § 2, 3°, namely levity in the pastor's way of life and infamy on the part of relatives, do not in themselves bring about infamy of fact. When the Code states, moreover, that infamy does not affect one's relatives, ". . . firmo praescripto can. 2147, § 2, 3°,"[84] this does not mean that canon 2147 constitutes an exception to the rule concerning infamy, as if to imply that canon 2147 actually adverts to the juridical notion of factual infamy. Canon 2293, § 4, is to be understood as asserting that in spite of the fact that neither infamy of fact nor infamy of law affects the relatives of the one who is infamous, the provisions of canon 2147, § 2, 3°, which does not really deal with infamy as such, must be observed as regards the removal of a pastor who will not dismiss from his household those who have performed some misdeed, and thereby have lost their good reputation.

Section 5. "Infamia facti contrahitur . . . APUD FIDELES PROBOS ET GRAVES. . . ."

That the loss of reputation be among Catholics (*fideles*), if there is to result an infamy of fact as the Church understands it, is a note added by the Code to the traditional concept of infamy of fact.[85] Equity prompted this inclusion, for if Catholics are to be barred from ecclesiastical acts and honors and from the sacraments because of the loss of their reputation, the defect should be noted among Catholics themselves. The Church should not be bound to consider the judgment of those who themselves do not belong to the Church in such matters as affect the lives of Catholics as Catholics.

In the early days of the Church it was more important to the

[84] "Neurta [infamia] afficit delinquentis consanguineos aut affines, firmo praescripto can. 2147, § 2, 3°."—canon 2293, § 4.

[85] Vogelpohl, p. 154.

overall growth of the Church that only those who were of good reputation among the pagans as well as among the Christians should be chosen for Orders. St. Paul accordingly, in writing to Timothy, said that a candidate for the episcopate ". . . must have a good reputation with those who are outside, that he may not fall into disgrace and into a snare of the devil."[86] Saint Luke, however, noted about Timothy himself that his good reputation was among Christians as well as among the pagans: "And behold, a certain disciple was there named Timothy, son of a believing Jewess, but of a Gentile father. And he was highly thought of by the brethren in Lystra and Iconium."[87]

Though Catholics are specified in our law today as those on whose judgment depends the loss of another's good name, the view of those outside the Church can certainly serve as adminicular proof for the ordinary,[88] especially in a community overwhelmingly non-Catholic and one in which these non-Catholics are themselves known to be good and serious people.

That the loss of reputation be among good and serious people is a just and ancient presupposition. It is just because only people who themselves attempt to live according to God's laws are qualified to judge regarding the character of others. An appreciation of virtue, a regard for the truth, the wisdom and ability to give rumors cautious hearing, are basic to the proper evaluation of a neghbor's reputation. It is an ancient presupposition because the phrase "*apud bonos et graves*" appears in the Roman law itself, in a connotation which has caused it to be cited as an example of infamy of fact.[89]

In the Decretals of Gregory IX, it was specified that the requirement of swearing to one's innocence according to the canonical form was consequent upon being defamed ". . . *apud bonos et graves. . . .*"[90]

---

[86] I Tim., 3, 7.

[87] Acts, 16, 1 and 2.

[88] Vogelpohl, p. 154.

[89] "Ea, quae pater testamento suo filios increpans scripsit, infames quidem filios iure non faciunt, sed *apud bonos et graves* opinionem eius, qui patri displicuit, onerant."—C. (2.11) 13.

[90] C. 15, X, *de purgatione canonica,* V, 34.

The glossators, too, made the adverse opinion of the good and serious people the foundation of infamy of fact.[91]

The law of the Decretals required that with regard to the number there had to be more than just a few of these good and serious people before there was actually infamy of fact.[92] Authors, however, have never estimated just how many good and serious people must think or speak ill of another before infamy of fact can or does attach to him. The Code, too, does not specify how many good and upright Catholics must lose respect for an individual before he becomes infamous by infamy of fact. Since, however, infamy of fact consists in a public loss of honor, and since public loss of honor is fundamentally a consequence of a public delict, the provisions of the Code in regard to publicity of delicts may be applied to infamy of fact.

In the Code a threefold distinction is made in regard to publicity; crimes may be public, or notorious by notoriety of law, or notorious by notoriety of fact.[93] A public delict is one which is already commonly known, or one in which the circumstances are such as to lead to the conclusion that it can and will easily become commonly known.[94] Only when the delict is already commonly known (*divulgata*) can it be said that infamy of fact is present. Even when the circumstances are such as to make one conclude that the crime will surely become commonly known in the future, infamy of fact is not present. A crime may, then, be public in the sense of canon 2197, 1°, and still not be one which has already brought on infamy for the delinquent. As soon as the crime does become commonly known, it is constituted as the kind of crime that brings on infamy of fact.

The extent to which this *divulgatio* must reach is difficult to determine. The Code itself does not state how many people must

---

[91] "Infamia facti est quando quis aggravatur vel infamatur apud bonos et graves."—*glossa ord.* ad c. 2, C. III, q. 7, *ad verbum "infamia."*

[92] "Qui [iudex] propter dicta paucorum eum infamatum reputare non debet, cuius apud bonos et graves laesa opinio non exsistit."—c. 21, X, *de accusationibus, inquisitionibus et denunciationibus,* V, 1.

[93] Canon 2197.

[94] Canon 2197, 1°.

known of a crime before it is *"divulgatum,"* but certainly if the majority of the people in a community, town, city or parish, or if in fact in any such group more than ten people know of the crime, it is "commonly known."[95] The notion of a public crime must moreover be considered in relation to the notion of an occult crime, since the Code states that an occult crime is one which is not public.[96] In view of this definition, it would be difficult to insist that the majority of a community, etc., would have to know about a crime before it is public. If one were to set such a requirement, one would have to say that if, for example, only forty per cent of the community knew of the crime, the crime would still be occult. This is inadmissible, for the authors usually insist that even in a large city the knowledge of a crime may be had by no more than eight people (unless they are close relatives or friends, in which case a greater number may know of the crime) if one is rightfully to claim that the crime is still occult.[97] Accordingly, to Coronata[98] the following doctrine of Santamaria seems too liberal, namely, that in a community of 100, the knowledge of fifteen would make the crime public; in a community of 1000, the knowledge of twenty, and in a community of 5000, the knowledge of as many as forty people.[99] These figures may, however, be employed as a norm for determining when a crime is public in such a way that infamy of fact is present. Since, however, infamy of fact is such a relative thing in view of the person and the circumstances involved, it is left to the ordinary to judge when a crime is public in the measure from which a loss of reputation for the delinquent results.

It is to be noted, however, that a crime must evince a specific type of publicity if infamy of fact is to be present; the crime must be public among good and serious-minded Catholics. When, there-

---

95 Coronata, *Institutiones,* IV, n. 1645, p. 13; Vermersch-Creusen, *Epitome,* III, n. 384, p. 221.

96 Canon 2197, 4°.

97 Coronata, *Institutiones,* IV, n. 1645, p. 14.

98 *Institutiones, ibid.,* note 4.

99 *Comentarios al Código Canónico* (6 vols., Madrid, 1919-1922), VI, 54.

fore, it is at times stated that a crime can be said to be public if only one or two particularly loquacious people know of the crime,[100] it is not only because of the limited number of the people who know of the crime, but also because of the imprudent character of these individuals, that infamy of fact is not present.

In the Code, notoriety is distinguished from publicity and itself is divided into factual notoriety and legal notoriety. A delict is notorious by notoriety of law after the sentence of a judge which has become a *res iudicata,*[101] or after the confession of the criminal made in court according to canon 1750.[102]

Delicts notorious by notoriety of law do not necessarily bring on infamy of fact, since they are not necessarily commonly known. A crime notorious by legal notoriety is *legally more serious* than a merely public crime, in so far as a crime is said to be notorious when the fact of the crime and its imputability are certainly known beyond any doubt. In another sense, a crime which is notorious by legal notoriety is *less serious* than a merely public crime, since there is not necessarily in a crime notorious by notoriety of law an actual divulgence among the people, nor the certainty that it will come later.[103]

It will often happen that those who are guilty of legally notorious delicts, i.e., after they have received the sentence of a judge or have confessed, will become infamous by infamy of fact through the observance of the penalty, for, although the law is most solicitous about preserving the good reputations of people, even

---

[100] Coronata, *Institutiones,* IV, n. 1645, p. 14.

[101] A *res iudicata* is had after two conformable decisions, or secondly, if the sentence when passed is not appealed within the time allowed by law, or though it was appealed before the judge *a quo,* was later abandoned before the judge *ad quem,* or thirdly, after one definitive sentence in a matter which according to canon 1880 does not allow for an appeal.—canon 1902.

[102] Canon 2197, 2°.

[103] "Delictum notorium est aliquid *amplius* et aliquid *minus* delicto publico; *aliquid amplius,* quia, ut tale habeatur, requiritur ut de eo iam certo constet et probationes habeantur non solum de facto sed etiam de imputabilitate. *Aliquid minus* quia, aliter ac in publico, in notorio delicto non requiritur nec actualis divulgato nec certa eiusdem praevisio."—Coronata, *Institutiones,* IV, 19.

of such as are guilty of crime, to the extent that it permits them not to observe the penalty they deserve when there is danger of infamy resulting from such an observance, ("... *quoties eam servare sine infamia nequit.* . . ."), this exception does not apply after a declaratory sentence, or if the delict is in any way notorious.[104]

A crime is notorious by notoriety of fact if it is publicly known and if in addition it was committed under such circumstances that no maneuver can conceal nor any legal defense excuse it.[105]

There are two elements in the definition of a factually notorious crime. The first element is the public knowledge of the crime, which links this type of crime with the public crime as it is described in the first number of canon 2197. While most of the authors merely repeat the wording of the Code, namely, that a factually notorious crime is one which is *"publice notum,"* Regatillo explicitly identifies it as a crime ". . . *quod iam est divulgatum.*" [106] Brys implies this too when he says that a factually notorious crime is something more than (rather than something different from) a public crime by reason of the certitude connected with a notorious crime.[107]

Coronata, however, says that a *delictum notorium* is not a species of the *delictum publicum,* and that the *publice notum* does not refer to the *iam divulgatum* of the definition of a public crime.[108] There does not seem to be any basis for such an assertion. In fact, it seems most reasonable to believe that factual notoriety is a species of publicity, the specific difference being supplied by the clause

---

[104] Canon 2232, § 1. Cf. *supra,* pp. 44-51.

[105] Canon 2197, 3°.

[106] *Institutiones Iuris Canonici* (4. ed., 2 vols., Sal Terrae: Santander, 1951), II, n. 78, p. 443.

[107] *Juris Canonici Compendium* (10. ed., 2 vols., Brugis: Desclée de Brouwer, et Sii, 1947-1949), II, 410.

[108] ". . . notitia publica non est, ut videtur, idem ac divulgatio et potest cum divulgatione concurrere, at non necessario cum ipso coniungitur. Publica notitia non necessario ad universum populum extenditur, sed ad paucas etiam personas restringi potest. . . ."—*Institutiones,* IV, p. 16, note 2. ". . . negamus quodlibet delictum notorium notorietate iuris aut facti debere necessario esse publicum ad mentem Codicis, quasi notorium esset species publici."—*loc, cit.,* n. 1647, p. 19,

following the *et* in the definition of factual notoriety, ". . . *and* committed in such circumstances that no maneuver can conceal nor any legal defense excuse it."[109] This certainty in a factually notorious crime arises from the manner and circumstances of the commission of the crime, whereas the certainty in a legally notorious crime arises from the legal means, a judicial sentence or legal confession, as they are mentioned in canon 2197, 2°. It is juridical certainty concerning a crime and its imputability which is proper to such notoriety.[110] The law attaches the notion of publicity to the factually notorious crimes because of the very way in which they are committed, which publicity will not necessarily be verified in cases of legally notorious crimes.

The certainty concerning the imputability which goes with crimes which are said to be factually notorious is not a necessary quality of a crime such as brings on infamy of fact. Crimes notorious by notoriety of fact can, certainly, cause infamy of fact, but so too can crimes which are simply public and which do not furnish the ultimate certainty as to the imputability of the delict that arises from the very circumstances in which the crime was committed. Both public crimes and those which are notorious by notoriety of fact can cause *infamia facti.*

The Code actually adverts to two distinct degrees of infamy of fact. The one demands notoriety, and the other calls for publicity, according to the meanings assigned these notes in canon 2197. Infamy with the note of notoriety is indicated in canon 855, § 1, wherein it is stated that the ". . . *manifestoque infames* . . ." are not to be allowed to receive Holy Communion. Manifestly infamous persons are actually notoriously infamous persons, for "manifest" adds the element of inexcusableness which makes public delinquents notorious ones.[111] The other cases of infamy in the Code do not

[109] *Notorium notorietate facti,* si publice notum sit et in talibus adiunctis commissum, ut nulla tergiversatione celari nulloque iuris suffragio excusari possit."—canon 2197, 3°.

[110] Vermeersch-Creusen, *Epitome,* III, n. 384.

[111] ". . . et 'manifesti' quia excusari nequent. . . ."—Blat, Lib. III, Partes II-VI, n. 104; "Manifeste aut manifesto significat in Codice illam certitudinem, quae attigit gradum notorietatis."—Oesterle, "Casus ad Canonem 855 C. J. C.," *Perfice Munus,* XIV (1939), 747. Cf. *infra,* pp. 96-97.

require the certainty regarding the crimes and the guilt of the delinquent that is required in this canon.[112]

Section 6. "Infamia facti contrahitur . . . DE QUO IUDICIUM SPECTAT AD ORDINARIUM."

The force of this clause is debated. Coronata makes the judgment of the ordinary essential to the incurring of infamy of fact; until the ordinary has judged in a case, infamy of fact has not been incurred, according to his opinion.[113] Vogelpohl follows the same view.[114] They go so far as to say, and Naz agrees with them in this,[115] that instead of judging in each case the ordinary may make his declaration before any crime is committed at all, by means of a diocesan law or statute.[116] This seems an erroneous interpretation of the clause, for thereby an application of the provisions in the penal law concerning *ferendae* and *latae sententiae* penalties is made to what the law contemplates as a factual loss of reputation and not a penalty.

Most of the authors take it for granted that the ordinary merely judges whether or not the other conditions in the description of infamy of fact are verified, so that infamy of fact can be known to be present in a given case. Thus Augustine (1872-1943),[117]

---

[112] Such public sinners who are also infamous by infamy of fact (cf. *supra*, pp. 52-53) are to be denied ecclesiastical burial only when they are manifestly, and therefore notoriously, public sinners.—canon 1242, § 1, 6°, which canon uses the expression "*peccatores publici et manifesti.*"

[113] "Declaratio autem Ordinarii necesaria omnino videtur ita ut nunquam quis infamia facti laborare censendus sit nisi declaratio precesserit."—*Institutiones,* IV, p. 268.

[114] *The Simple Impediments to Holy Orders,* p. 155.

[115] *Traité de Droit Canonique* (4 vols., Parisiis: Letouzey et Ané, 1946-1948), IV, 685 (hereafter cited as Naz).

[116] "Nec necessaria videtur singulis in casibus sententia aut declaratio Ordinarii, sed sufficere declaratio lege dioecesana aut statuto lata."—Coronata *Institutiones,* IV, 268; Vogelpohl, p. 159.

[117] "Infamy of fact exists when one, by reason of a crime committed, or on account of a bad character, has lost his good reputation with upright and serious Catholics. *Whether and when this is the case, is for the Ordinary to decide.*"—Augustine, VIII, 245.

Chelodi (1880-1922)—Ciprotti[118] and Berutti[119] exemplify this position.

Latini (1857-1938) pointed out that it is simply not in the power of a judge to impose infamy of fact, or to cause it to exist by his judgment. He asserted that infamy of fact is beyond the scope of a judge's power, that is to say, infamy of fact is not determined by any judicial procedure, but is the object of the ordinary's administrative procedure.[120] When, in the matter of infamy of fact, therefore, reference is made to the ordinary as "judge" and to his decisions as "judgments," it is in the administrative and not the judicial sense that these words are to be understood.

The term "ordinary," inasmuch as the law does not specify the local ordinary, includes abbots and prelates *nullius,* vicars general, diocesan administrators, vicars apostolic, prefects apostolic, the legitimate successors during the vacancies of these offices, and major superiors of exempt clerical religious.[121] These are the proper persons to determine whether or not a person is infamous, and whether that infamy is serious enough to warrant the restrictions stated in the law regarding the persons involved. These, too, are the proper superiors to determine when the infamy has been sufficiently removed to allow for the lifting of these restrictions.[122] By their judgment they do not automatically cause people to think better or worse of an individual, but rather determine when popular opinion is bad and when it is not.

Must the ordinary be consulted in every case? That is not demanded by the Code. When a law bars those who are infamous from being sponsors at baptism and confirmation,[123] and from the

[118] ". . . Ordinarii est iudicare quando adsit."—*De Delictis,* n. 50, p. 66.

[119] "Ordinarii loci est in singulis casibus prudenter iudicare num quis reapse infamia facti laborare eiusdemque proinde effectibus subiici legitime censendus sit. . . ."—*De Delictis,* p. 220.

[120] *Iuris Criminalis Philosophici Summa Lineamenta* (Taurini, 1924), p. 200.

[121] Canon 198, § 1.

[122] Canon 2295.

[123] Canons 766, 2°; 795, 2°.

reception of Holy Communion,[124] it seems obvious that the ordinary's judgment cannot reasonably be demanded for each and every case. His judgment should be obtained in the case of one to be ordained,[125] since it is the ordinary's responsibility to judge regarding the fitness of the candidates for Orders, and the absence of any irregularities and impediments, such as infamy of fact.[126] The ordinary should also be the judge in each case involving the reception of ecclesiastical dignities, benefices and offices and the exercise of the sacred ministry,[127] and of certain authorized ecclesiastical acts, such as administering ecclesiastical goods, taking part in ecclesiastical trials, voting in ecclesiastical elections, and exercising the right of patronage.[128]

In cases which are involved in the pastor's care of the souls in his own parish and in the administration of sacraments in the parish, the ordinary need not judge regarding the presence of infamy in every case. Rather the pastor who is presumed to know his flock,[129] as also the circumstances of his parish, important in any judgment concerning them, and who has by law the responsibility of administering the sacraments properly,[130] is ordinarily the proper one to determine whether a person is infamous and, therefore, unworthy to act as sponsor at baptism or confirmation, and to receive Holy Communion.[131] If the pastor is challenged in this matter, or if there be some doubt whether infamy of fact is actually present or whether the effects of infamy necessarily apply in a given case, then surely the ordinary should be consulted and his judgment, as based on the facts presented to him, is to be followed. The ordinary is the proper one to solve every real doubt in this matter of infamy of fact.

If the pastor cannot be consulted because he is simply not available, or if there is not enough time to approach him in the matter,

---

124 Canon 855, § 1.

125 Canons 987, 7°; 2294, § 2.

126 Canons 968; 987, 7°; cf. *infra,* pp. 110-118.

127 Canon 2294, § 2; cf. *infra,* pp. 123-131.

128 Canons 2294, § 2; 2256, § 2; cf. *infra,* pp. 131-136.

129 Canon 467, § 1.

130 Canon 462.

131 Canons 766, 2°; 795, 2°; 855.

any priest may and very often must make a prudent judgment on his own as to the presenec of infamy. Thus the assistant, if he be alone at the parish church at the time when a child is brought for baptism, must himself forbid one who has lost his good reputation in the parish to act as a sponsor.

The judgment of the ordinary when it is required will be based on the answers to many questions: What is the basis for the loss of reputation of the person involved? It is a serious basis? What is the status of the person involved? How important and how well known is he in the community? Has he lost his reputation among many people? Are they good people? Are they Catholics? What percentage of the people in the locale are non-Catholics? How important to the good of the Church in that place is their judgment? If some of those who accuse him are non-Catholics, what is their status among the Catholics? Is the accused person really guilty of that of which he is accused? If guilty, how serious is his offense in his own community in which he now lives? Was it actually committed in the place where he now lives? If loss of reputation is the result of suspicion with reference to some crime or evil deeds, is there a firm basis for the suspicion? Can the suspicion be easily disproved?

After considering such questions the ordinary judges concerning the person involved. Should he judge that the person is infamous in fact, the effects of infamy of fact will be binding upon the infamous person throughout the territory in which the ordinary has jurisdiction, or throughout as much of it as the ordinary determines. Thus a person infamous in one parish may perhaps not have to be denied the reception of Holy Communion in another parish of the same city, or in another part of the diocese in which he is unknown. It is even more possible that someone infamous in one diocese, and determined to be such by the ordinary of that diocese, will be well thought of in another diocese. The ordinary of the second diocese will have to determine whether the effects of infamy hold for the person there, after considering the danger of detection of the person's bad reputation elsewhere and of consequent scandal.

CHAPTER III

The Investigation and Cessation of Infamy of Fact

Article I. The Investigation of Infamy

The Code makes little mention of any investigation of infamy of fact, though such investigations are necessary from the very nature of infamy. Doubts, suspicions and accusations being involved as often as they are, only by investigations can the ordinary resolve the doubts and determine whether or not a person is infamous. The law, then, assigns to the ordinary the obligation of investigating a matter wherein infamy may be involved when it makes the ordinary the judge as to the existence or cessation of infamy of fact.[1]

Such an obligation also arises from the overall duty on the part of the episcopal ordinary to see to it that there are no abuses of ecclesiastical discipline among his subjects, and that purity of conduct in the clergy and laity is preserved.[2]

The bishop is not the only one who may make the investigation. Since it is the judgment of the "ordinary" that is demanded by law in the determination of infamy, anyone who comes under the comprehensive term "ordinary" in the sense of the Code may conduct the necessary investigation. The vicar general, therefore, could inquire into the possibility of infamy in a given case, as could the major religious superiors and the others mentioned in canon 198, § 1. Such officials as the diocesan chancellor do not have the right by reason of their office to undertake investigations concerning infamy. If the ordinary has authorized them to do so, they do of course have the proper power and should carry out the investigation according to the instructions of the ordinary, and in secret as far as this is possible.[3]

The bishop also deals with the clerics of his diocese through the

[1] Canons 2293, § 3; 2295.

[2] Canon 336, § 2.

[3] Canon 364, § 2, 3°.

vicar forane appointed by him as a supervisor of the clerics in a district of the diocese.[4] The vicars forane are to observe whether or not the clerics are leading a life in conformity with canon law.[5] Included in this commission, certainly, is the right and the obligation to make an investigation concerning any matter which is serious enough to involve loss of reputation on the part of a cleric.

A report concerning such matters should be submitted by the vicar forane to the ordinary at least once a year.[6] The law states that a report should be made *at least* once a year. Cases of a more serious nature should, of course, be brought to the ordinary's attention as soon as they are detected, and since infamy of fact is a serious loss of reputation based on a delict or corrupt morals, the ordinary should as soon as possible be advised of the possibility that infamy has been contracted by a cleric of the diocese. It also seems proper that the ordinary should be informed about such a possibility, for the reason that, since it is the ordinary's obligation to judge concerning the presence of infamy, he himself is the proper one to determine the nature and extent of the investigation concerning infamy.

When officials who by common law or delegation are not given the right to make an investigation concerning infamy among clerics nevertheless undertake to do so, the clerics have the right of not responding. Only to the ordinary and his delegates must they respond. It is the obligation of replying that is spoken of here, for often clerics who supposedly are infamous will not object to replying to superiors other than their ordinaries.

The pastor is fully within his rights in investigating this matter with reference to the laity in his parish. When, however, the investigation concerns a layman whose infamy may have consequences beyond the parish in which he has his domicile, the ordinary of the diocese should be informed.

It will usually happen that the ordinary will conduct the investi-

---

[4] Canons 217; 447, § 1, 1°.

[5] "Vicario foraneo . . . ius et officium est vigilandi . . . num ecclesiastici viri sui ambitus seu districtus vitam ducant ad normam sacrorum canonum suisque officiis diligenter satisfaciant. . . ."—canon 447, § 1, 1°.

[6] Canon 449.

gation concerning infamy as each case is presented to him. Beyond this practice, however, an excellent opportunity for inquiring into the possibility of infamy is provided the ordinary in the episcopal visitation of his diocese.[7] This visitation will furnish occasion for the ordinary to learn to known all the people, so that he may make better provisions for their spiritual good, as the II Plenary Council of Baltimore (1866) noted.[8] Their spiritual good and that of the whole Church will be served by the detection and uprooting of any practice among Catholics that entails for them a loss of respect among the righteous Catholics of the locality. Some of the things which may easily cause infamy and therefore may be the concern of the visiting bishop are the prevalence of cremation, civil marriages, public concubinage, mixed marriages, membership of lay Catholics in non-Catholic organizations, in masonic lodges, in other forbidden societies, in socialistic and communistic parties, etc.[9]

If the bishop neglects the visitation of his diocese which he is obliged to make in accordance with canons 343-346, the metropolitan can and must supply the neglect after having obtained the approbation of the Holy See.[10] On the occasion of this visitation, the metropolitan may preach, hear confessions, absolve from cases reserved to the local bishop, and make inquiries into the life and character of the clergy. He is also to denounce to their ordinaries the clerics marked with infamy so that their deserved punishment may be measured out to them.[11] The metropolitan himself may punish notorious crimes, and manifest and notorious offenses against himself or his retinue, with just penalties, not exclusive of censures.[12]

---

[7] Canons 343-346.

[8] *Concilii Plenarii Baltimorensis II Acta et Decreta, 1886* (2. ed., Baltimorae: J. Murphy, 1894), n. 86.

[9] Slavkosky, *The Canonical Episcopal Visitation of the Diocese,* The Catholic University of America Canon Law Studies, n. 142 (Washington, D. C.: The Catholic University of America Press, 1941), p. 134.

[10] Canon 274, 5°.

[11] "*. . . potest . . . clericos infamia notatos Ordinariis ipsorum, ut eos puniant, denuntiare. . . .*"—canon 274, 5°

[12] *Loc. cit.*

Although infamy of fact is obviously indicated in the right of denunciation accorded to the metropolitan, it is not obvious that infamy of law is excluded. Both types of infamy, therefore, may be considered as envisaged in the canon here cited.[13]

The metropolitan obviously has the right to determine whether infamy of fact is present since he is supplying for the ordinary who for some reason or other has neglected to make the called for judgment. The metropolitan does not have the right to punish those who are marked with infamy. The law explicitly states he is to *denounce* them to their ordinaries in order that the latter may punish those who are infamous. This is also obvious from the fact that the law distinguishes between the infamous whom the metropolitan is to *denounce* and the ones guilty of notorious crimes whom he himself may *punish.* This denunciation, however, is not a mere formality; the ordinaries are to heed it by punishing the guilty clerics or else the ordinaries are disregarding a strict obligation.[14]

The metropolitan, furthermore, has the right to notify the Roman Pontiff concerning the matter in accordance with canon law no matter what actions the ordinary may take or fail to take.[15]

The denunciation of infamous persons by the metropolitan is limited by the law to infamous *clerics.* It seems reasonable, however, that if he detect infamy among the laity he will bring this to the attention of the proper ordinary. Popek appeals to canon 19 in this matter, and requires a strict interpretation of canon 274, 4°, [16] since a penalty is stated in this latter canon.[17] But no viola-

[13] Blat, Lib. II, p. 292; Popek, *The Rights and Obligations of Metropolitans,* The Catholic University of America Canon Law Studies, n. 260 (Washington, D. C.: The Catholic University of America Press, 1947), p. 238 (hereafter cited as Popek).

[14] Popek, *loc. cit.*

[15] "In diocesibus vero suffraganeis Metropolita potest . . . vigilare ut fides disciplina ecclesiastica accurate serventur, ac de abusibus Romanum Pontificem certiorem facere."—canon 274, 4°.

[16] *Op. cit.,* p. 240.

[17] The metropolitan denounces the infamous clerics to their ordinaries that they, the ordinaries, may punish these infamous clerics ("*ut eos puniant*").

tion of canon 19 seems involved if in this matter lay people are also contemplated for while the infamous clerics are denounced precisely that they may be punished, the infamous lay people are not necessarily denounced with the same purpose in view. If the metropolitan insisted upon such punishment for the latter, the ordinary would be acting within his rights, so it seems, if he did not comply with the metropolitan's demand. The purpose of the metropolitan's denunciation of the infamous laity is that the ordinary may be properly informed about his subjects, and that he may act on this information in the manner and at the time he judges it expedient to do so.

The metropolitan has the right to denounce all clerics secular and religious except those who enjoy the privilege of exemption according to canon 615. Infamous religious are not thus exempted from the metropolitan's denunciation, a), if they are illegitimately outside their house, or b), if they have not been duly corrected and punished by their proper superior or by the ordinary of the place, who should have informed the Holy See concerning the superior's neglect in this matter.[18]

The metropolitan should denounce the infamous religious to the exempt religious superior, since canon 274, 4°, uses the expression *"Ordinariis ipsorum,"* and not *"Ordinariis locorum."* The metropolitan must, however, inform the ordinary of the place, if the crime was committed outside of the religious house and the religious was not punished by his proper superior, since canon 616 obliges the ordinary of the place to take cognizance of such matters. Lastly, the metropolitan may inform the Holy See by reason of the ruling contained in canon 274, 4°, and canon 616. It seems that he is also *obliged* to inform the Holy See, since that is the obligation of the ordinary of the place for whose neglect the metropolitan is here supplying.

Besides the general investigations concerning infamy as mentioned or at least presumed by law, there are two specific types of investigation which may involve infamy: 1) the investigation of candidates for Orders by the ordinary with regard to their good

[18] Canons 616 and 617.

reputation, which investigation is made through the pastor of the candidates,[19] and 2) the prenuptial investigation by the proper pastors concerning impediments and public sinfulness.[20]

Article II. The Cessation of Infamy

Canon 2295.—*Infamia iuris desinit sola dispensatione a Sede Apostolica concessa; infamia facti cum bona existimatio apud fideles probos et graves, omnibus perpensis adiunctis et praesertim diuturna rei emendatione, fuerit, prudenti Ordinarii iudicio, recuperata.*

Infamy of law is a vindicative penalty. As is the case with all such penalties, it is removed by means of a dispensation.[21] Canon 2295 states that this dispensation is to be granted by the Holy See. Upon the granting of this dispensation the penalty is lifted, and at the same time the irregularity which accompanied it ceases. The penalty and the irregularity are imposed by the law, and so

---

[19] S. C. de Sacramentis, 27 dec. 1930—*AAS*, XXIII, p. 120; Bouscaren, *The Canon Law Digest* (2 vols. and supplement through 1948, Milwaukee, Wisc.: The Bruce Publishing Co., 1934-1943-1949), I, n. 8, p. 267 (hereafter cited as *Digest*).

[20] Canons 1020 and 1066. Public sinners who have at the same time lost their reputation are dealt with here. Donovan says concerning them: "Though canons 1065 and 1066, which mention these two classes of unworthy Catholics, form part of the chapter of the Code on the prohibitive impediments, the restrictions of which these two canons treat do not, according to the better opinion of canonists, constitute any matrimonial impediments in the strictly canonical sense." Concerning the investigation into this matter, he says: "The Ordinary will have to depend on the information of the pastor for the forming of his judgment concerning the gravity of the cause. Consequently, the pastor has the duty of determining what the cause is and of correctly informing the Ordinary."—Donovan, *The Pastor's Obligation in Pre-Nuptial Investigation,* The Catholic University of America Canon Law Studies, n. 115 (Washington, D. C.: The Catholic University of America, 1938), pp. 269 and 275; cf. the Instruction, "Examination of the Parties to be Conducted by the Pastor at a Suitable Time Before the Marriage"—S. C. de Sacramentis, 29 iun. 1941, n. 8—*AAS,* XXXIII (1941), 297; Bouscaren, *Digest,* II, 267.

[21] Canon 2236, § 1.

they are removed through the process of the law. In this sense, infamy of law actually reflects an artificial loss of reputation. One may incur such a legal loss of reputation through the commission of a crime to which the penalty is attached *ipso facto,* without anyone's knowing of the crime or of one's incurring of the penalty. Though the dispensation of the penalty is reserved to the Holy See, the rule on this point refers only to public cases. In occult cases of infamy a dispensation may be granted by the ordinary, acting either personally or through delegates.[22]

Public and notorious delicts which involve infamy of law will very often lead to infamy of fact as well. The removal, however, of the infamy of law by way of a dispensation will not necessarily effect the cessation of infamy of fact. Infamy of fact is a real loss of reputation among good and serious-minded people, and only when the lost reputation has been regained can one say that infamy of fact has ceased. Rather than say, then, that infamy of fact is removed, it is preferable to say that it ceases or that one's good name is restored.

The impediment consequent upon infamy of fact is not co-extensive with it as is the irregularity that is connected with infamy of law, i.e., it is possible for one to be infamous by infamy of fact in one locality without being impeded from ordination or the exercise of Orders in another locality.[23] The impediment arising from the infamy can be removed by a change of domicile, but not the infamy itself.[24] Thus, in the principal decisions of the Sacred Congregation of the Council concerning infamy of fact, it is invariably stressed that the penance imposed for the cessation of infamy

---

[22] Canon 2237, § 2.

[23] Vogelpohl, p. 162.

[24] It is true, in a sense, that infamy ceases by a change in domicile, since the upright people who once thought ill of another cease to think of him at all when he has moved away to another place. Moralists, then, speak of a change in residence as a way in which infamy ceases, e.g., Prümmer, & Co., 1923) III, n. 618, p. 422; Bucceroni, *Institutiones Theologiae Moralis* (6. ed., 4 vols., Romae, 1914-1915), IV, n. 1347, p. 347. It is better to say that infamy ceases *as an impediment* in the new domicile which the person acquires before it ceases as a fact.

should be performed in the place where the infamy originated, and not in some other place.[25]

Infamy of fact as well as the impediment ceases, as the Code says,[26] when one's good reputation has been restored, and the principal way in which this is accomplished is through a long period of amendment and penance, which, of course, must be publicly known to the people among whom the reputation was lost. It is said that the performance of the penance must be publicly known, and not that the performance of it must be of the nature of a public penance, so that the life of penance could be evinced outside of the community in which the person lost his good name, as long as those who are of the community know that the penance has truly been performed.

This period of amendment and penance may be entered into by the infamous person on his own initiative, or he may be ordered to do so by his superior. The place for the performance of the penance is to be determined by the ordinary. As has been said, it may be performed within the community or the parish which is the present residence of the one who is infamous, or it may be performed outside of that community, even outside of that diocese, provided that the ordinary of the diocese to which the infamous person is to come has given his consent, which in certain instances may be presumed, as when an ordinary has established or permitted the establishment of an institution for the rehabilitating of such people as need it. It is, in fact, most commendable that the persons of bad reputation, and especially clerics and religious, perform their penance in a religious atmosphere among people dedicated to the meritorious and splendid task of assisting them to

[25] S.C.C., *Spoletana,* 19 ian. 1737—*Fontes,* n. 3467; S.C.C., *Elboren.,* 9 febr., 16 mart. 1737—*Fontes,* n. 3470; S.C.C., *Salernitana,* 9 febr. 1760—*Fontes,* n. 3693; S.C.C., *Terulen.,* 3 iul. 1762—*Fontes,* n. 3720; S.C.C., *Terulen.,* 27 aug., 24 sept. 1763—*Fontes,* n. 3731; S.C.C., *Agrigentina,* 10 dec. 1767, 16 et 30 ian. 1768—*Fontes,* n. 3759; S.C.C., *Sabinen.,* 20 maii, 17 iun. 1786—*Fontes,* n. 3853; S.C.C., *Nullius Montis Virginis,* 16 febr., 5 apr. 1788—*Fontes,* n. 3858; S.C.C., *S. Miniati,* 20 mart. 1830—*Fontes,* n. 4029; S.C.C., *Civitatis Castelli,* 11 mart. 1843—*Fontes,* n. 4082; S.C.C., *Ferrarien.,* 25 ian. 1851—*Fontes,* n. 4116.

[26] Canon 2295.

atone for their past and to strengthen them spiritually for the future. These places may also provide an opportunity for the proper treatment of such disorders as alcoholism and dope addiction.

The duration of the period of penance is not specified in law, since, as far as the matter of infamy is concerned, it should last as long as it takes to effect a change in the status of the reputation of the infamous person. The ordinary is to judge when a sufficient period of penance has been observed. He may lengthen it beyond the time of emendation required for the cessation of infamy, namely as a punishment according to the nature and gravity of the crimes committed.[27] It is the mind of the Holy See, however, that an ordinary deal paternally and benignly with his priests as befits a good shepherd in relation to the select of his flock even while taking into account that the public good and the spiritual well-being of a priest himself call for an amendment of life and some punishment when infamy is involved.[28]

While an absolute norm for the duration of the period of amendment is ruled out by the fact that *infamia facti* is so relative a matter, there is certainly great precedent for the extension of the penitential period to three years. This is the duration upon which the Sacred Congregation of the Council has based many of its decisions concerning the cessation of infamy.[29] Saint Alphonsus (1696-1787) cited Viva (1648-1726) and La Croix (1652-1714)

---

[27] This is especially true when scandal has been caused, or when there is a special gravity or heinousness in the transgression, in which cases a broad power of punishing is given to superiors in canon 2222, § 1.

[28] This is evidenced in an instruction of the Sacred Consistorial Congregation in regard to priests who in the course of military service have committed some major crime: "Cum clericis in sacris, qui forte in aliquod ex maioribus delictis, durante militari servito misere lapsi forent, quum redeunt, Ordinarii paterne quidem se gerant, sed ad eorum emendationem et salutem et in publicum Ecclesiae bonum, non omittent in singulis casibus iuxta criminum naturam procedere, prout in lib. V Codicis praescribitur, praesertim si in infamiam iuris vel facti incurrerint. Cum iis vero qui per lugendum nefas a suis votis vel etiam a religione apostatae ad saecularem statum transiverint, iidem Ordinarii boni pastoris officium, quantum in ipsis est, agere non omittant, errantes oves opportune quaerendo." Cf. S. C. Consist., 25 oct. 1918—*AAS,* X (1918), 486.

[29] *Supra,* p. 76, note 25.

as authors who had regarded it as the common opinion that three years were necessary as the minimum period of amendment for the regaining of one's good reputation.[30]

Vogelpohl says that a three-year period of amendment suffices to meet the requirements of the law.[31] Coronata,[32] Naz,[33] and Woywod (1880-1941)[34] claim that there is an analogy between canon 672, § 1, which speaks of a *plena emendatio per triennium* in regard to dismissed religious who seek a return to religion,[35] and canon 2295 which deals with the cessation of infamy of fact. Other authors require at least a two-year period of amendment for the restoration of one's good name.[36]

While this norm which calls for a period of two or three years provides us with the traditional notion regarding the duration of the amendment, there is no obligation at all to accept that norm, since the Code has not specified any period of time in this matter. Canon 672, which by way of an analogy is cited by certain recent authors, seems to pertain little or not at all to infamy of fact. The author in *Il Monitore* stated that even a shorter time could suffice for the removal of infamy, and advocated what the Code now states as law, namely that it pertains entirely to the ordinary to decide how long a period of time is required for the cessation both of the infamy and of the impediment.[37] His judgment will be based on the nature of the crime or sinful actions, the degree of publicity

---

[30] *Theologia Moralis* (4 vols., ed. Gaudé, Romae, 1905-1912), lib. VII, cap. V, dub. IV, n. 364, p. 467.

[31] *The Simple Impediments to Holy Orders,* p. 160.

[32] *Institutiones,* IV, n. 1828, p. 269.

[33] *Traité du Droit Canonique,* IV, n. 1102, p. 685.

[34] *A Practical Commentary,* II, pp. 504-505.

[35] Canon 672, § 1—"Dismissus, votis in religione emissis non solutus, tenetur ad claustra redire; et si argumenta plenae emendationis per rationes sive ex parte religionis sive ex parte religiosi, res iudicio Sedis Apostolicae subiiciatur."

[36] Berutti, *De Delictis,* p. 226; cf. "Intorno alla irregolarità che si contrae colla infamia," *Il Monitore Ecclesiastico,* X, Parte II (1898), 16.

[37] "Noi crederemmo che possa talevolta anche in minor tempo alcuno purgarsi di un delitto con prove di pentenza più conspicua e più efficace; imperocchè non essendo questa vera irregolarità, come si è detto innanzi, sta al superiore il giudicare quando alcuno possa aver riguadagnata la stima presso il pubblico."—*Loc. cit.*

attaching to the acts, the status of the delinquent before the loss of his good name, the goodness of the people of the community in which the penance and amendment take place, and upon the public nature of the penitent's acts of virtue.[38] Even a relatively shorter period of time than that which some authors require for this amendment, even six months, for instance, may well be long enough ot serve the purpose of regaining the good reputation of someone who lost it for some minor crime.

Baptism has also been proposed as a way in which infamy of fact ceases. The glossators were the first to present this effect of baptism.[39] There were, however, reservations to this means of ridding oneself of infamy; the infamy which arose from certain grave crimes of sacrilege and simony, for instance the murder of a priest, the burning of a church, the purchase of a religious house, were too serious to permit the return of one's good reputation solely through baptism or even upon a period of penance.[40] Saint Alphonsus included baptism as a means of bringing about the cessation of infamy of fact.[41] Suarez taught it as the common opinion that infamy was removed by baptism, and pointed out that this referred to infamy of fact and not to infamy of law, since the non-baptized were not subject to Canon Law.[42] Gasparri admitted that baptism effected the cessation of infamy of fact at times, but not always.[43]

Authors since the Code make no mention of baptism as a means whereby infamy ceases to exist. The Code specifies that after all

[38] Vogelpohl, p. 160.

[39] *Glossa ord.*, c. 99, D. IV, *de cons.*, *ad verba "in baptismate"; glossa ord.*, c. 3, D. XXVI: "I claim that infamy and the irregularity arising from one's own delict are taken away in baptism, for the gifts of baptism are granted without the requirement of penance or satisfaction. . . . This is evidently the case with Saint Paul, who before baptism was guilty of murder, yet afterward was made an Apostle . . .,"—*ad verba "inter peccata."*

[40] Guido a Baisio, *Commentaria in Decretorum Volumen*, p. 157, on c. 39, C. II, q. 7.

[41] *Theologia Moralis*, Lib. VII, n. 364.

[42] Suarez, *Omnia Opera* (Vivès editio, ed. Carolus Berton, 26 vols., Parisiis, 1856-1861), Vol. XXIII (*De Censuris*, pars I, disp. XLVIII, sec. II, nn. 12-13), p. 520.

[43] *De Sacra Ordinatione*, I, n. 310, p. 200.

circumstances are considered, especially a long period of amendment, the ordinary is to judge whether one's good reputation has been restored. This statement of the law shows the stress which is to be placed on the amendment of life over and above all other considerations. Baptism, accordingly, while its reception may actually do much to win the esteem of good Catholics toward a sometime infamous but recently converted person, does not rule out the necessity of a period of amendment. This, at least, seems to be logically deducible from the emphasis which the law puts on the *diuturna rei emendatio.*

Repentance, amendment and satisfaction for scandal are required by canon 855 if those who were infamous are to be allowed to receive Holy Communion. This poses several problems which are dealt with in the section devoted to this sacrament.[44] It suffices here to note that Oesterle divides these infamous persons into two categories, those who live sinfully in the sense that they live in a certain permanent state of sin, such as concubines, or persons invalidly married, and those who live sinfully in the sense that they perform oft-repeated gravely sinful acts, such as drunkards and blasphemers.[45] Persons in this second group can be admitted to Holy Communion if they previously receive the sacrament of penance. The confessor will have required the penitent to live publicly the life proper for a Christian. Persons of the first category, however, must make further amendment.

For those who have lost their reputation unjustly, as through false accusations or any unjust sentence, it is not necessary that a period of penance be entered into. It would, actually, be wrong to have them do such a thing, since it would only serve to convince people who had already been misled, and to persuade others who had previously withheld judgment, that this innocent person was actually guilty of that of which he had been accused or convicted. What is required is a declaration of innocence by his ordinary and the civil authorities (as by means of a pardon), if that is also necessary. If in such a case a judge has caused a person

---

[44] *Infra*, pp. 98-110.

[45] Oesterle, "Casus ad Canonem 855 C.J.C.", *Perfice Munus*, XIV, (1939), 746-747.

to become infamous by his decision, he should attempt to effect a return of that person's former good status by rescinding his first decision,[46] or by recommending a pardon by the proper executive authority.

In all of these matters the judgment of the ordinary is to prevail. It is he who judges when the good reputation of a person has been restored, when sufficient penance has been performed, when the person involved may return to or take up the offices, functions, ecclesiastical acts, etc., from which he had been barred. The ordinary may consult the Holy See about what procedure should be taken in a particular case of infamy, but he is not obliged to do so. It seems preferable, therefore, that he deal with each case according to its own circumstances. General legislation. then, as in diocesan statutes, would little serve the ordinary in the handling of these matters.

The ordinary's judgment counts, of course, throughout his own territory, and each ordinary will have to judge for himself even when one and the same person is involved. Against the judgment of the ordinary a recourse may be invoked by one who had good reasons to expect a favorable response from the ordinary. Several of the decisions of the Sacred Congregation of the Council, as cited earlier in this article, were favorable responses to such appellants.

While the rendering of a judgment by the ordinary is not necessary for the actual cessation of the infamy, it is necessary for the cessation of the legal effects of the infamy. This judgment is presumed or implied in the call to Orders or in the appointment by the ordinary to an office, benefice or exercise of the sacred ministry from which the appointee had previously, as one infamous, been barred.[47]

---

[46] Sanctus Alphonsus, *Theologia Moralis*, Lib. VII, n. 364.

[47] Coronata, *Institutiones*, IV, n. 1828, p. 269; Vogelpohl, p. 163.

CHAPTER IV

The Effects of Infamy of Fact as Regards the Sacraments

Article I. Sponsors at Baptism and Confirmation

The Church has always expected that only men and women of the highest character should act as sponsors at baptism and confirmation. In its legislation the Church accordingly demands the goodness in these people which befits the spiritual parentage which the function of sponsorship includes, so that Pope St. Nicholas (858-867) said: "A person should love as a father the one who took him from the holy font."[1] To merit such love the godparents have traditionally assumed and undertaken great obligations:

> Above all, I warn you, women as well as men, who have taken up children in baptism, remember that you have stood as sponsors before God for those whom you decided to take up from the sacred font. Hence, exhort them continually to keep chaste, to love justice, to cultivate charity. Above all keep the Creed and the Lord's Prayer yourselves, and manifest them to those whom you have received as spiritual children.[2]

The assertion of these noble duties the Code has repeated for us today.

> It is the godparents' duty, arising from the office they have undertaken, to regard their spiritual child as their perpetual charge, and in the things which regard the obligations of the Christian life to see to it with all diligence that their godchild may in all relations of life prove himself such as they pledged that he should be when they stood sponsor for him in the solemn ceremony.[3]

---

[1] C. 1, C. XXX, q. 3.

[2] C. 105, D. IV, *de cons.*

[3] Canon 769.

Among those who are not permitted to exercise the function of sponsorship at baptism and confirmation the Church includes those who are infamous, in order to prevent those who have not fulfilled their own spiritual duties from being placed in a position where they will be responsible for the spiritual duties of others, and, secondly, in order to prevent scandal from arising as might be the case should the office be given to one of bad repute, and, thirdly, in order to punish somewhat the ones who recklessly brought about the loss of their own good reputation.

Sponsorship in connection with these sacraments reflects a most ancient practice, which probably dates back to the very earliest administration of the two sacraments. Tertullian around the year 200 spoke of sponsorship in such wise as to indicate that it was of common usage in his time.[4] A sponsor at baptism served as sponsor for confirmation as well, for confirmation was conferred immediately after the subject had received baptism, and as part of his rite of initiation into membership in the Church.[5]

As early as the fourth and fifth centuries rural churches in the West had already begun to deviate from the traditional practice of administering these two sacraments together.[6] The Council of Compiègne (756) gave evidence that sponsorship at confirmation was continued even after the introduction of the practice of administering this sacrament independently of the sacrament of baptism, when it stated that whosoever acted as godparent for his own

---

[4] *Tractatus de Baptismo,* cap. XVIII—Migne, *Patrologiae Cursus Completus, Series Latina* (221 vols., Parisiis, 1844-1855), I, 1221 (hereafter cited as *MPL*).

[5] *Ibid.,* cap. VII et VIII: "Egressi de lavacro perungimur benedicta unctione. . . . Dehinc manus imponitur per benedictionem advocans et invitans Spiritum Sanctum."—*MPL,* I, 1206.

[6] St. Jerome (ca. 342-420) said that it was customary for the bishop to visit distant communities to confirm those who already were baptized by the priests or deacons. Cf. *Dialogus adversus Luciferanos*—*MPL,* XXIII, 164. Furthermore, Innocent I (401-417) stated that those who baptized either in the absence or in the presence of the bishop were allowed to anoint with chrism those whom they baptized provided the chrism was consecrated by the bishop; but they were not to mark the forehead with the same oil, since that was the privilege of bishops alone when they communicated the Holy Ghost.—*MPL,* XX, 555.

child while the bishop administered confirmation was to be separated from his spouse and was not to marry another.[7] Bennington is of the conviction, accordingly, that ". . . godparents had been employed in this sacrament from the time that its conferral first became separated from the rite of baptism."[8] What is required for sponsors in baptism is required for sponsors in confirmation, as is clear from the very nature of their functions and the attendant historical developments.

From the first, surely, only persons with unblemished reputations were permitted to assist in the role of spiritual parents at these rites wherein first all spiritual blemishes were removed from the newly born in Christ, and then the strength of the Holy Spirit was given them to help to prevent further blemishes. St. Augustine (356-430) said of the sopnsors that they were to be *"boni fideles,"* and this he said parenthetically, taking it for granted, so it seems, that they were orthodox believers known in their community to be people of upright life and good repute.[9]

In 829, a provision of the VIII Council of Paris (of that same year) was included in the "Episcoporum ad Hludovicum Imperatorem Relatio," in the Capitularies of the Frankish Kings. This provision excluded those who were excommunicated and those who were undergoing public penance (and therefore infamous by reason of infamy of fact) from the function of sponsors at baptism and at confirmation:

> We declare, though, that they especially are to be denied this office who are excommunicated and who are subjected to public penance, so that they may not be the ones who will

---

[7] Canon XII: "Si quis filiastrum aut filiastram ante episcopum ad confirmationem tenuerit, separetur ab uxore sua et alteram non accipiat."—Hardouin, *Acta Conciliorum et Epistolae decretales ac Constitutiones Summorum Pontificum* (12 vols., Parisiis, 1714-1715), III, 2005 (hereafter cited as Hardouin).

[8] *The Recipient of Confirmation,* The Catholic University of America Canon Law Studies, n. 267 (Washington, D. C.: The Catholic University of America Press, 1952), p. 35.

[9] *Ep.* XCVIII [*ad Bonifatium,* ca. 408]—*MPL,* XXXIII, 361-362.

> receive others from the baptismal font, or act as sponsors for others at their reception of the gifts of the Holy Ghost.[10]

The I Provincial Council of Milan in 1565 warned parents to pick as sponsors those who by reason of their upright lives (*"ratione morum"*) would be able to fulfill the function of spiritual paternity or maternity.[11]

In 1614, Pope Paul V authorized the publication of the *Rituale Romanum.* What the earlier Councils had established it confirmed as the necessary qualifications of those who were to function as sponsors and it laid on the pastor the obligation to determine whether the sponsors were worthy and fit to act as sponsors, both at baptism and at confirmation.[12]

There are two provisions in the Code concerning infamy and sponsorship at baptism. By reason of canons 795, 2°, and 796, 3° these provisions pertain to sponsorship at confirmation also. The first,

> *Ut quis sit patrinus, oportet . . . ad nullam pertineat haereticam aut schismaticam sectam, nec sententia condemnatoria vel declaratoria sit excommunicatus aut infamis infamia iuris aut exclusus ab actibus legitimis, nec sit clericus depositus vel degradatus.*—canon 765, 2°,

is a requirement which pertains to infamy of law and not to infamy of fact, and is one which must be verified in order that a person may *validly* be a sponsor. The second requirement involves both infamy of fact and also infamy of law in a qualified sense and is to be verified in order that one may *licitly* be a sponsor; it reads:

---

[10] *MGH,* Legum Sectio II, *Capitularia Regum Francorum,* (Vol. II, Pars I, denuo ediderunt A. Boretius et V. Krause, Hannoverae, 1890), c. 35, p. 39.

[11] Mansi, XXXIV, 16.

[12] *Rituale Romanum Pauli V Pontificis Maximi iussu editum, et Benedicti XIV auctum et castigatum* (3. ed., Neo Eboraci, 1882), Tit. II, cap. 1, nn. 22-26 (hereafter cited as *Rituale Romanum Pauli V*).

> *Ut autem quis licite patrinus admitiatur, oportet . . . non sit propter notorium delictum excommunicatus vel exclusus ab actibus legitimis vel infamis infamia iuris, quin tamen sententia intercesserit, nec sit interdictus aut alias publice criminosus vel infamis infamia facti.*—canon 766, 2°.

If contrary to the law, therefore, one who is infamous by reason of infamy of fact acts as sponsor at baptism or confirmation, he does so validly and is actually a godparent of the one who received the sacrament. Accordingly such a person has the obligations which go with that office.

There is a question of some importance concerning canon 766, 2°, namely whether or not the expression *"propter notorium delictum"* refers to the *"infamous infamia facti"* in that same number. The importance rests in the fact that, since notorious crimes are of a much more specific nature than merely public crimes, there are more cases of infamy of fact rising from crimes which are simply public than from those which are classified as "notorious."[13] If the phrase concerning notorious crimes qualifies those who are infamous by infamy of fact, then fewer people are prevented from acting as sponsor than would be prevented if the law does not restrict the notion of infamy, which can be caused simply by public crimes as well as by notorious ones.[14] The very construction of the sentence indicates that *"propter notorium delictum"* does not refer to *"infamis infamia facti."* There are two sections in the sentence, the first one beginning with *"non sit,"*[15] and the other with

---

[13] *Supra,* pp. 60-65.

[14] Delicts which simply are public are more common than notorious crimes by reason of the fact that they need only to be *commonly known* in order to be classified as "public." The *certainty* of the commission of a crime and its imputability pertain to notorious crimes and not to those which simply are public. *Supra,* pp. 62-64.

[15] In this section the lawgiver considers a certain group collectively, because they were just considered in the previous canon, 765, 2°; there it is stated that the ones who under the accompaniment of a declaratory or condemnatory sentence are punished with excommuniction, with infamy of law, or with exclusion from the legally authorized acts, are incapable of *validly* becoming sponsors. In canon 766, 2°, it is stated that those people who incur these penalties apart from the accompaniment of a condemnatory or a declaratory sentence may not *licitly* act as sponsors.

"nec sit," which negative conjunction is used for the introduction of an entirely separate thought. The phrase, *"propter notorium delictum,"* and the clause, *"quin tamen sententia intercesserit,"* which occur in the first part of the sentence are not to be carried over to the second part of the sentence, wherein the law adverts to infamy of fact. Crimes which simply are public, therefore, even though they have not the additional note of certainty that is proper to crimes which are called notorious by notoriety of fact, are the crimes that entail the *infamia facti* as it is envisaged in canon 766, 2°.

In the second part of canon 766, 2°, ". . . *nec sit interdictus aut alias publice criminosus vel infamis infamia facti,"* the *"publice criminosus"* and the *"infamis infamia facti"* go together by reason of the conjunction *"vel,"* as distinct from the *"interdictus,"* from which they are dissociated by means of the particle *"aut"*.[16] Blat accordingly says that the infamy, here, is by reason of the *publicitas* (and not therefore the *notorietas*) of canon 2197.[17] The expressions "public criminals" and "persons infamous by infamy of fact" frequently have the same extension in meaning, but this is not necessarily so, since the delict of the public criminal may not yet be commonly known, but simply may have been committed in such circumstances that it can be prudently judged that it can and will easily become known in the future. It is only when the crime actually becomes commonly known that the one who committed it becomes infamous.[18] There is, accordingly, good reason for including both of these expressions.

Many authors, however, demand notoriety as an essential element of the infamy of fact which keeps the infamous from licitly

---

[16] *"Vel"* is a conjunction which connects things similar because they allow of alternation; *"aut"* connects things which do not allow of such alternation.—E. A. Andrews, *A Copious and Critical Latin-English Lexicon* (New York, 1874), p. 181, s. v. *"aut."*

[17] ". . . 'publice' *criminosus;* et ex c. 2197: 'Delictum est publicum, si iam divulgatum est aut talibus contigit seu versatur in adiunctis ut prudenter iudicari possit et debeat facile divulgatum iri'; quae publicitas extat quoque in sequenti: c.) *vel infamis infamia facti. . . ."—Commentarium,* Lib. III, Pars I, 61.

[18] *Supra,* p. 60.

acting as godparents.[19] In the light of what has been said above, this requirement of notoriety seems to go beyond what is demanded by the Code itself.

Prümmer and Abbo-Hannan do not include such public sinners as drunkards among the infamous who are barred from sponsorship.[20] These people may, however, be considered infamous "... *ob pravos mores.*" At any rate, to say as Prümmer said,[21] that it is permissible to permit such unworthy people as drunkards and those who fail to make their Easter duty to be sponsors, because the duty of their office (namely to supervise the spiritual education of the godchildren) is not a serious requirement any more, is definitely far from the mind of the Church as reflected in the following statement:

> And this (the duty of sponsors to look to the Christian education of their spiritual children) is to be insisted on more strongly in our times, when faith and morals are more in danger, and when parents themselves sometimes forgetting their grave obligations fail to care as they should for the

[19] Prümmer says of those who are listed in canon 766, 2°: "Haec omnia possunt breviter comprehendi; illicite admittuntur ad patrini officium publici peccatores, ut iam in Rituali Romano erat."—*Manuale Iuris Canonici,* p. 374. The reference here is to that list which in the Roman Ritual prior to 1925 included the *"manifestoque infames"* (the notoriously infamous), such as prostitutes, concubines, usurers, magicians, fortune-tellers and blasphemers.—Cf. *infra,* p. 95. Regatillo also says that the infamy of fact as now mentioned in canon 766, 2°, is the same as the notorious infamy mentioned in the Roman Ritual prior to 1925.—*Ius Sacramentarium,* I, 42. Naz even more explicitly demands notoriety in the delictual act both of the *"publice criminosus"* and of the *"infamis infamia facti"*: "De même, nous avons traduit le publice criminosus du can. 766, par 'pécheur notoire', et non 'pécheur public,' nous croyons qu'il s'agit de quelqu'un vivant en état de péché d'une façon notoire de fait. L'infamie de fait (can. 2293, § 3) ne peut être encourré que pour des actes réels et personnels; pratiquement elle suppose aussi la notoriété de fait de ces faits. Nous insistons sur cette notion de notoriété, parce qu'elle seule permet l'enquête rapide que suppose le Code."—*Traité de Droit Canonique,* II, 47.

[20] Prümmer, *Manuale Theologiae Moralis,* III, 109; Abbo-Hannan, *The Sacred Canons* (2 vols., St. Louis: Herder, 1952), I, 767 (hereafter cited as Abbo-Hannan).

[21] *Manuale Theologiae Moralis,* III, 109.

> Christian education of their children; and hence the services of the sponsors are to be rendered all the more diligently. . . . But today when faith is growing cold, this sacred sponsorship established of old by the Church is despised or made little of. . . . But this evil, so grave and so shameful to Christian manhood, must be entirely removed; there must be a return to obedience to the mind of Holy Mother Church. . . .[22]

Those who are punished with exclusion from the authorized ecclesiastical acts are included in the list of canon 766 among those who are barred from licitly acting as sponsors, if they incurred the punishment apart from the accompaniment of any declaratory or condemnatory sentence.[23]. Actually, the inclusion of this class of delinquents in canon 766 was not necessary, for the reason simply that sponsorship is already mentioned elsewhere in the Code as one of the authorized ecclesiastical acts, and anyone who is barred from them collectively will be barred from any one of them, individually, sponsorship included.[24]

The impediment to marriage which ordinarily arises between the minister and the baptized, and also between the sponsor and the baptized, arises even though the sponsorship came about illicitly, as would be the case if the sponsor were infamous by infamy of fact.[25]

In a case of doubt whether a person can act as sponsor either validly or licitly, the pastor should consult the ordinary, if there is time.[26] The time needed for this communication between the pastor and the ordinary is to be computed according to the usual time required for the making of a personal journey or the exchange

---

[22] S. C. de Sacramentis, 25 nov. 1925—*AAS,* XVIII (1925), 47; Bouscaren, *Digest,* I, 343-344.

[23] Automatic incurrence of this penalty is enacted in the common law in canons 2315, 2350, § 2, and 2357, § 2. It is otherwise incurred after the pronouncement of sentence; cf. canons 2353; 2375; 2385. After such a sentence they cannot *validly* become sponsors.—canon 765, 2°.

[24] Canon 2256, 2°.

[25] Wernz-Vidal, *Ius Canonicum,* Vol. IV, Pars I, p. 47; Cappello, *De Sacramentis,* V, 529.

[26] Canon 767.

of letters.[27] The recourse must be had whether the doubt is one of law or one of fact.[28] It is for the ordinary to decide whether or not infamy is present, and whether or not the person in question should be allowed to act as sponsor. If there is not enough time for such recourse, the pastor or the one who takes his place must make both of the decisions himself.

If the pastor decides that the person who has presented himself to act as a sponsor is infamous, the prohibition of the law should ordinarily be made known to this person in an effective manner. The pastor may himself appoint another to act as sponsor, for the law gives him the power to do so, if the one who is to receive the sacrament, or his parents or guardians, fail to do so, or if, as when an infant is the recipient of the sacrament, he has no parents or guardians to make the choice for him.[29]. The failure of parents or guardians to present a suitable person as sponsor is tantamount to their failure to provide any sponsor at all.[30] Could the minister himself act as sponsor? The Code clearly supposes that the sponsor and the minister are two distinct persons, but since it does not explicitly state the contrary, the minister could act simultaneously as sponsor.[31] The minister of baptism, however, ordinarily a cleric in Sacred Orders,[32] must have the express per-

---

[27] Kearney, *Sponsors at Baptism According to The Code of Canon Law,* The Catholic University of America Canon Law Studies, n. 30 (Washington, D. C.: The Catholic University of America, 1925), p. 102.

[28] Canon 15 states that in a doubt of law, ecclesiastical laws are not binding. Here in canon 767, however, the pastor is obliged to have recourse to the ordinary, if time allows, even in a doubt of law, because what the pastor considers to be a doubt of law may not actually be a doubt of law at all. If the ordinary judges that such a doubt is present in the case presented to him, the individual in question should be allowed to assume sponsorship. Cappello offers such an explanation in regard to doubtful impediments to marriage.—*De Sacramentis,* V, 205. Cf. Kearney, *loc. cit.;* Blat, III, 60.

[29] Canon 765, 4°.

[30] Waldron, *The Minister of Baptism,* The Catholic University of America Canon Law Studies, n. 170 (Washington, D. C.: The Catholic University of America Press, 1942), p. 160 (hereafter cited as Waldron).

[31] Waldron, p. 161; Woywod, *A Practical Commentary,* I, 393-394.

[32] "Minister ordinarius baptismi sollemnis est sacerdos. . . ."—canon 738, § 1; cf. also canons 741; 744.

mission of his own ordinary to act as sponsor.[33] As regards the bishop as the minister of confirmation, although the Sacred Congregation for the Propagation of the Faith declared that he could not act as the sponsor and minister at the same time,[34] the Congregation of Sacred Rites later in a response to the Bishop of Policastro, Italy, permitted it if the bishop appointed a proxy to represent him as sponsor.[35] If for any reason and with the required permission a priest-minister of baptism acts also as sponsor, it is advisable for him to act through a proxy, as must the bishop-minister of confirmation.[36]

If the alternative to having one who is infamous act as sponsor at baptism be that of the priest-minister acting in that capacity, several things must be taken into consideration:

1) Both are forbidden by law to act as sponsor (unless the priest has the ordinary's permission so to act);

2) If no suitable sponsor can be had, the minister may simply baptize without one; the *"quantum fieri possit"* which relates to the obligation of obtaining a sponsor suggests that there can be such an exception to the general rule;[37]

3) If it is foreseen that grave inconveniences and grave harm to souls and to the Church would arise out of the refusal to allow a certain unsuitable person, (i.e., one who does not measure up to the requirements for licitness), to act as sponsor, the pastor should consult the ordinary. If the ordinary judges that these conditions are verified in the case presented to him, he may, according to a decision of the Sacred Penitentiary, allow the otherwise unsuitable person to assume sponsorship.[38] In view of this decision it seems that in such a situation as is here under consideration it would be

---

[33] Canon 766, 5°.

[34] 21 sept. 1843—*Collectanea S. Congregationis de Propaganda Fide* (2 vols., Romae, 1907), I, n. 969.

[35] S. C. Rit., 14 iun. 1873—*Fontes,* n. 6059.

[36] Waldron, p. 161.

[37] Canon 762, § 1; Waldron, p. 161.

[38] S. Poenit., 10 dec. 1860—*Fontes,* n. 6426; cf. Cappello: "Lex ecclesiastica non obligat cum gravi incommodo, ideoque parochus non tenetur repellere indignos, quos sine gravi damno nequit reiicere."—*De Sacramentis,* II, 156.

better for the minister to allow the unsuitable person proposed by the subject of baptism, or by the parents or the guardians, to act as sponsor rather than it would for the minister to do so himself. If the pastor has no time to consult the ordinary on whether he should allow the unfit person to become a sponsor in view of the harm which would result from refusing him this office, the pastor himself may decide to allow the party in question to be a sponsor. The pastor should make every effort to obviate any possible scandal, and should he foresee that it cannot be obviated, he would be obliged in charity to forbid the infamous person to be a sponsor, in spite of any consequent harm of a lesser degree than the impending scandal. If the pastor permits the unsuitable person to become a sponsor, he should make a special effort to explain to him the obligations of this function.

When the minister must deny an infamous person the role of sponsor, he should do so with as high a degree of charity and prudence as is possible.[39]

If the pastor has any reason to believe that the person proposed as sponsor is actually infamous, he is obliged to make inquiry concerning this. The obligation is even greater in regard to one who is unknown to the pastor and who is assuming sponsorship through a proxy. Thus the Sacred Congregation of the Sacraments has declared:

> For just as no one should be admitted by his pastor to the office of sponsor, who is not qualified for it by the conditions which are required for the valid and licit assumption of this office, so too, whenever in the conferring of the sacrament some one plays the part of sponsor, not in his own name but in the name and by the authority of some other certain and determinate person, it is necessary that this authority or the will of the person giving the authority be lawfully proved, . . so that the pastor may be able to investigate whether the designated sponsor has the qualifications required by law. . . .[40]

---

[39] Prümmer, *Manuale Iuris Canonici*, p. 374.

[40] S.C. de Sacramentis, 25 nov. 1925—*AAS*, XVIII (1925), 46-47; Bouscaren, *Digest*, I, 342.

Article II. Infamous Persons as Unworthy Recipients of Holy Communion

Can. 855, § 1—*Arcendi sunt ab Eucharistia publice indigni, quales sunt excommunicati, interdicti manifestoque infames, nisi de eorum poenitentia et emendatione constet et publico scandalo prius satisfecerint.*

§ 2. *Occultos vero peccatores, si occulte petant et eos non emendatos agnoverit, minister repellat; non autem, si publice petant et sine scandalo ipsos praeterire nequeat.*

Section 1. The Nature of this Infamy

Among the ones publicly known to be unworthy of receiving Holy Communion the Code includes those who are manifestly infamous. They have lost their good reputations for some reason, and until they have regained their good reputations they are not to be permitted the reception of this sacrament. The Code demands in effect the cessation of infamy when it demands repentance, amendment of life, and satisfaction for scandal caused, for the cessation of infamy is the proper effect of the acts.

There is question here of a certain habitual state of unworthiness, and not of the actual state of unworthiness such as is involved when one immodestly dressed or one in a state of drunkenness approaches the Communion rail. They are to be denied the Sacrament they seek, in view of being *"publice indigni"* of whom canon 855 makes mention, but not necessarily in view of identification with the *"manifestoque infames"* mentioned in the same canon.

Commentators and moral theologians usually deal with those who are publicly unworthy and those who are infamous under the title of "the sacraments in general."[41] The discussion regarding the

[41] Aertnys-Damen, *Theologia Moralis* (15. ed., 2 vols., Taurini: Marietti, 1947), II, 21-23. Sanctus Alphonsus, *Theologia Moralis,* Lib. VI, n. 44; Bucceroni, *Institutiones Theologiae Moralis,* III, 240; Cappello, *De Sacramentis,* I, 52-58; Coronata, *De Sacramentis Tractatus Canonicus* (3 vols., Taurini-Romae: Marietti, 1943-1946), I, 46-51 (hereafter cited *De Sacramentis*); Ferreres-Mondria, *Compendium Theologiae Moralis* (17. ed., 2 vols., Barcinone: Subirana, 1949-1950), II, 155-156; Genicot-Salsmans, *In-*

denial of the sacraments to the unworthy admittedly pertains most especially to the Eucharist.[42]

The Code bars from the reception of Holy Communion the publicly unworthy, i.e., not simply those who are known to have committed sins, but rather those whose unworthiness is exceptionally scandalous.[43] This is evident from the types of unworthy persons mentioned in canon 855. The excommunicated are named, though elsewhere they are forbidden to receive or administer any of the sacraments.[44] The *interdicti* included in the canon are also generally prohibited from receiving or administering all of the sacraments.[45] The *manifestoque infames,* however, demand a special consideration in this work. As to the kind of infamy involved, whether it be that of law or that of fact, or of both types together the law is not precise, nor do authors discuss the question generally. Rather they deal with this infamy as an infamy of fact, prescinding from any legal infamy. Some authors do say in passing that both infamy of law and infamy of fact are envisaged in this canon.[46] Other authors seem quite certain that only infamy

---

stitutiones Theologiae Moralis (17. ed., quam paravit Gortebecke, 2 vols., Bruxellis: Dewit, 1951), II, 18 (hereafter cited as Genicot-Salsmans); Iorio, *Theologia Moralis* (3. ed., 3 vols., Neapoli: D'Auria, 1946-1947), III, 15 (hereafter cited as Iorio); Lehmkuhl, *Theologia Moralis* (9. ed., 2 vols., Friburgi Brisgoviae, 1898) II, 29 (hereafter cited as Lehmkuhl); Merkelbach, *Summa Theologiae Moralis,* III, 82; Piscetta-Gennaro, *Elementa Theologiae Moralis* (5. ed., 7 vols., Taurini: Società Editrice Internazionale, 1941-1943), V, n. 81 (hereafter cited as Piscetta-Gennaro); Prümmer, *Manuale Theologiae Moralis,* III, 63-67; Regatillo, *Ius Sacramentarium,* I, 176-177.

[42] Piscetta-Gennaro, *loc. cit.;* Lehmkuhl, *loc. cit.;* Genicot-Salsman, *loc. cit.*

[43] "*Publice* indignus vel peccator *stricte* est solus cuius indignitas vel peccatum communiter noscitur; *minus stricte,* ut in § 1, peccator non vulgaris sed extraordinarius, scandalosus, ut ex allatis exemplis patet. Rituale ante a. 1925 inter infames, per modum exempli, recensebat usurarios, magos, sortilegos, blasphemos."—Regatillo, *Ius Sacramentarium,* I, 176.

[44] Canon 2261.

[45] Canon 2275.

[46] Stadler, *Frequent Holy Communion,* The Catholic University of America Canon Law Studies, n. 263 (Washington, D. C.: The Catholic University of America Press, 1947), p. 58 (hereafter cited as Stadler). It

of fact is involved. Thus Piscetta-Gennaro adopt the proposition of Genicot-Salsmans, who identify the infamy that is delineated in canon 855 as infamy of fact.[47]

Ayrinhac-Lydon say that when the infamy of law is publicly known (and is, therefore, infamy of fact as well), the infamous are to be known from the reception of Communion.[48] Kurczynski also lists this exclusion as an effect of infamy of law.[49]

It seems clear that both infamy of law and infamy of fact are envisaged in the canon under consideration. This is evidenced by the fact that the canon is taken from the Roman Ritual in use prior to 1925, which, in a provision pertinent to the unworthy and the reception of Holy Communion, listed as examples of infamy six crimes,[50] many of which in the earlier law carried with them the penalty of infamy, i.e., infamy of law: prostitution, concubinage,[51] usury,[52] magic and fortune-telling,[53] and blasphemy.[54] Although the Code does not repeat the listing of the

---

should be pointed out, however, that although this author states: "Also to be refused Holy Communion are those persons who have incurred the penalty of infamy, whether in law or in fact," infamy of fact is not a penalty.

[47] Genicot-Salsman: "Et canon 855, § 1, expresse iubet ab Eucharistia arceri excommunicatos, utique vitandos vel denunciatos, interdictos, denunciatos manifestoque infames—nempe qui tales evaserint quia ob patratum delictum vel ob pravos mores, bonam existimationem apud fideles probos et graves amiserint. . . ."—*Institutiones Theologiae Moralis,* II, n. 122; Piscetta-Gennaro, V, n. 84.

[48] *Penal Legislation in the New Code of Canon Law* (revised by P. J. Lydon, New York: Benziger Brothers, 1936), p. 122.

[49] *De Natura et Observantia Poenarum Latae Sententiae,* p. 156.

[50] ". . . manifestoque infames ut meretrices, concubinarii, feneratores, magi, sortilegi, blasphemi, et alii eius generis peccatores. . . ."—*Rituale Romanum Pauli V,* Tit. IV, cap. 1, n. 8.

[51] C. 9, C. III, q. 5, and c. 4, C. XXXV, q. 6, dealt with adultery, and c. 4, X, *de bigamis non ordinandis,* I, 21, and the constitution of Benedict XIV *"Dei miseratione,"* 3 nov. 1741—*Fontes,* n. 318, dealt with bigamy.

[52] C. 2, C. III, q. 7; c. 11. X, *de excessibus praelatorum,* V, 31. See also Alexander III, in cc. 1-3, X, *de usuris,* V, 19.

[53] C. 9, C. III, q. 5; c. 17, C. VI, q. 1.

[54] Leo X (in Conc. Lateranen. V), const. *Supernae dispositionis,* 15

Ritual, this omission does not mean that the lawgiver intended to exclude infamy of law. The Ritual included mention of certain criminals in brackets merely as instances of the type of infamous people who were meant to be included in the comprehension of the term "infamous," namely those who were most likely to be notorious sinners and unworthy to receive Holy Communion. There was really no need to include this listing of the Ritual, and the omission of that list is certainly not a discrepancy between the present and the earlier law, and therefore there is no reason for departing from the probable interpretation of the older law.[55]

The infamous persons mentioned in the Ritual by way of example were those who, by the very nature of their wrongdoings, would be known beyond all doubt to be unworthy of the reception of the sacraments. For the most part they were people whose sinfulness was their way of life. Those who were given to the practice of such ways of life as prostitution, the working of black magic, fortune-telling, usurious businesses, or any notoriously illicit professions, could be presumed to be infamous in fact.

Furthermore, the list given in the Ritual was not an exhaustive list as was plainly indicated there.[56] Others whose public sinfulness was so notorious as that of the ones listed were also to be excluded from the reception of Holy Communion. This is true also in the present law by reason of the *"ob pravos mores"* in the description of infamy of fact.

The *"manifestoque"* of the canon and the Ritual denotes that notorious crimes and sins are indicated; *"manifestus"* in its various forms in the Code invariably refers to notoriety, and not simply to publicity.[57] That these infamous persons must be notoriously

---

maii 1514—*Fontes,* n. 65; S. Pius V, const. *Cum primum,* 1 apr. 1566—*Fontes,* n. 111; S.C.C., *Terulen.,* 27 aug., 24 sept. 1763—*Fontes,* n. 3731.

[55] Cf. canon 6, 3°.

[56] ". . . et alii eius generis peccatores."—*loc. cit.*

[57] Canons 54, § 1; 1323, § 3; 1905; 1921, § 2; cf. *supra,* p. 64. Iorio offers the singular opinion that notorious and public are sometimes synonymous, and that this obtains in the matter with which we are dealing here: "Adverte tamen quod "notorium" quandoque sumitur pro omnino publico, i.e. eodem sensu qui a Codice tribuitur delicto notorio ad normam can. 2197. Quo in casu inter *publicum* et *notorium* non tenet distinctio de qua

such means that there must be more than mere suspicion and rumor about their guilt. There must be some certainty that a definite person has committed some crime commonly known to have been perpetrated, or is living habitually in sin or in the occasion of serious sin. The crimes or sins may or may not be notorious by law (after the sentence of a judge or the culprit's confession in court), but they must be notorious in fact, i.e., publicly known and so committed that there does not remain any possibility for excusing them or explaining them away by means of any legal defenses.[58] Notorious crimes and sins are obviously spoken of here not abstractly, but rather in reference to certain persons who as a result of these crimes are barred from the reception of the Eucharist as persons manifestly or notoriously infamous. The authors are consistent in their demand for this mark of notoriety in reference to public sinners.[59]

The notoriety here postulated does not at all conflict with the classification of *public* sinners under which it is included, for while "public" and "notorious" are distinguished in canon 2197, "public" here in canon 855 is taken in a generic sense, broad enough to include the notoriously infamous as an example of just what public sinners are meant. For notorious sinners are not necessarily public ones; legally notorious sinners may actually be known to but a few people and not to the public.[60]

The ones here considered as notoriously infamous are those and only those who are publicly and commonly known to be such. It is obvious, then, that the infamous mentioned in canon 855 are

---

hic et in dubio sequenti."—*Theologia Moralis,* III, n. 27, p. 15. The Code in canon 2197 does not make "*public*" and "*notorious*" equivalent terms, but rather declares that a notorious delict is a more specific type of delict than is a public delict. A delict notorious by notoriety of fact is one which is publicy known and which has been committeed in such circumstances that no maneuver can conceal nor any legal defense excuse it; cf. *supra,* pp. 63-64.

[58] Canon 2197, 2°, 3°.

[59] Stadler, p. 58; Prümmer, *Manuale Theologiae Moralis,* III, 63; Van Hove, *Tractatus de Sanctissima Eucharistia* (2. ed., Mechliniae: H. Dessain, 1941), p. 163.

[60] *Supra,* p. 62.

invariably infamous by reason of infamy of fact, no matter whether or not they have contracted the penalty of legal infamy. Those who are infamous by infamy of law are included only to the extent that they are also infamous in fact, and moreover notoriously so. Those who are infamous by infamy of fact, whether infamy of law accompanies it or not, must always be notoriously and not simply publicly infamous.

The public sinners who are notoriously infamous in the sense of canon 855 have two chief characteristics: 1) they commit exceptionally serious sins or crimes; 2) they cause scandal which must be removed and remedied before they can receive Communion.[61] One other characteristic, however, may be noted. According to the notion of infamy of fact in the Code of Canon Law, the public knowledge of the unworthiness of the public sinner must exist among Catholics.[62]

Section 2. The Cessation of this Infamy

In order to bring about the cessation of such infamy as prevents one from receiving Communion, the Code repeats the demands of the Roman Ritual prior to 1925 in requiring: 1) repentance (*poenitentia*); 2) amendment (*emendatio*); and 3) public satisfaction for any scandal given. These acts are in general the acts which together with the actual confession of sins combine to make up the matter of the sacrament of penance.[63] Since, however, infamy of fact connotes a public state of unworthiness, it is required here that the acts mentioned in canon 855 also be somewhat public in nature. In this way such acts assist in the setting aside of a person's unworthiness in the external forum just as they neutralize his unworthiness in the internal forum.

Thus repentance (*poenitentia*) is in itself an interior disposition of sorrow for one's sins. Even this repentance, when infamy of fact is involved, should be made public. It is considered that there is

---

[61] "Publice indignus vel peccator [in 855, § 1] . . . est . . . peccator non vulgaris, sed extraordinarius, scandalosus, ut ex allatis exemplis patet [videlicet in Rituali Romano]."—Regatillo, *Ius Sacramentarium,* I, 176.

[62] Canon 2293, § 3; cf. *supra,* p. 58.

[63] Noldin, *De Sacramentis,* III, p. 254.

repentance enough when the public sinner receives the sacrament of penance. He should receive this sacrament publicly, that is to say, he should enter the confessional before many people, or at least before enough to warrant the presumption that his repentance will be made known to those among whom his unworthiness is already known.[64] This will generally be sufficient to remove entirely the public unworthiness of those who are unworthy because of some oft-repeated sins or crimes committed in public, but who are not placed in any proximate occasion of sin and who have not given rise to excessive scandal.[65] There are actually many who will come under this provision, people who have blasphemed repeatedly and publicly in the past, those who have often drunk to excess, or who have habitually dressed immodestly, etc. They have sinned grievously and publicly, and as a consequence may have become infamous. Sinners of this type, however, show by their reception of the sacrament of penance, as long as it is voluntary, that they have the purpose of amendment, and wish to repair the scandal which they have caused, and among Catholics of good will that will actually be accomplished through such a reception of penance.[66]

These former sinners approach the Communion rail not as sinful people but as penitent people, and thereby edify rather than scandalize the rest who are present, so that the Council of Auch in France in 1851 pronounced: *"Saepe enim ipsa sacramenti receptione sufficiens praebetur scandali reparatio."*[67] The confessor should, this same Council said, make suggestions as to how the scandal should be repaired, which will always include living up to one's public obligations as a Catholic.[68]

---

[64] Lehmkuhl, II, 31; Merkelbach, III, 82.

[65] [Alii auctores] . . . dicunt sufficere confessionem coram pluribus. . . . Et recte Croix adhaeret huic sententiae, quando peccator non habet proximam peccandi occasionem: quia qui publice confessus est, publice censetur emendatus; secus, si adesset occasio, et ille eam non deseruerit." —Bucceroni, *Institutiones Theologiae Moralis,* III, 242; Lehmkuhl, *loc. cit.*

[66] Oesterle, "Casus ad Canonem 855 C.J.C.," *Perfice Munus,* XIV (1939), 747.

[67] *Acta et Decreta Sacrorum Conciliorum Recentiorum, Collectio Lacensis* (7 vols., Friburgi Brisgoviae, 1890-1892), IV, 1183, ad 70.

[68] *Op. cit.,* IV, 170, cap. VIII.

If, therefore, a person was once a public sinner but has not offered any great scandal, and if now he is in no permanent occasion of sin, this person should, after a public appearance at the confessional, be granted the reception of the Most Blessed Sacrament. While his sins were serious and public, there is a presumption which mature Catholics must make, namely that real sorrow prompted his reception of the sacrament of penance, and that the grace from that sacrament and from the reception of Holy Communion will strengthen his resolve to effect a change from his former sinful practices.[69]

Amendment (*emendatio*) here denotes a public indication of a conversion from a sinful way of life to one which is pleasing to God. This amendment is required for those infamous persons who live in a certain permanent state of sin, as concubines, or whose sins are reflected in the external forum until at least some act, e.g., of reconciliation, restitution or cessation from coercion, has been promised and performed.[70]

Corrupt politicians, and those employers and professional men who are notoriously lacking in justice are included here, as are those who are engaged in gravely sinful occupations, offices or businesses, as usurers, harlots, panderers, fortune-tellers, and pracTioners of black magic.[71] Persons living in invalid marriages are likewise included among those who must make an amendment of their lives. This is true because of the scandal which is given by these sinners, or the scandal which would be given if such people

[69] Blasphemers have been mentioned above as coming under the category of public sinners treated in this regard. Bucceroni said of them, and presumably of others who were listed with them above, that even if they have not publicly gone to confession, they may be presumed to have done so, and so may be given Holy Communion when they publicly request it.—*Institutiones Theologiae Moralis,* III, 242. This, however, seems less than what canon 855 requires in this matter.

[70] Oesterle, *loc. cit.*

[71] "Black magic" is that harmful superstitious magic which is distinguished from harmless "white magic," as it is called by moralists. "Alia est magia alba seu naturalis, quae definitur ars operandi mira et insolita per media naturalia; alia est magia nigra seu superstitiosa, quae definitur ars operandi mira ope daemonis. Etiam magia cum daemonis invocatione explicita vel implicita fieri potest."—Noldin-Schmitt, II, 160.

were to be permitted the reception of the Most Blessed Sacrament. Since it is in view of the scandal caused that these infamous persons are barred from the sacraments, even those people who are supposedly infamous, though actually they are not guilty or at least not as guilty as people believe them to be, are still to be denied the sacraments and the ecclesiastical offices, benefices and functions listed in canon 2294, § 2.

This amendment of life and the third requirement of canon 855, the public satisfaction for scandal, will often go together. The amendment of life, while in itself it involves the cessation and renunciation of a sinful practice or occupation, or the leaving of some occasion of sin, will usually include satisfaction for the scandal caused by the sinful practice or occasion of sin, because of the necessarily public nature of such an act of amendment. It must be clear, however, that there is intended a conversion or a return to a good way of life, and that the former godless way of life has been abandoned for noble reasons and not for worldly ones, such as the desire for promotion or prestige, or for the winning of an election. The amendment of life, in order to satisfy for the scandal, must not only be of a public nature, but must also be publicly known to be sincere.

The amendment of life, in order to cause the infamy of fact to cease, must extend over a long period of time.[72] The exact significance of the *diuturna emendatio* generally required for the cessation of infamy of fact in regard to canon 855 is not easily discerned. A special problem arises in this regard. The frequent and fervent reception of the Blessed Sacrament is in itself the great means of gaining the grace to lead a good life. It also serves as an indication to other Catholics that one is trying to please God and to atone for past offenses against Him. The reception of Holy Communion is, then, a way of amendment, and of regaining one's good reputation.[73] Canon 855 seems to demand that those infamous persons

---

[72] *Supra,* pp. 76-79.

[73] This is especially exemplified in a canon of the *Decretum* of Gratian, which canon he took from a Council of Worms held in 868. The canon provided that in the event of a theft in a monastery the monks were to prove their innocence through the reception of Holy Comunion according

who are still public sinners or who at least are still in the occasion of sin are not to be given Communion. Those, then, who have publicly renounced their wrongdoings, as could be done by those who separate after they had lived in a notoriously invalid union, though they have not as yet regained their good reputations in the neighborhood, may be admitted to the reception of Communion not only occultly but even publicly. By receiving the Blessed Sacrament they may sooner regain their good reputations. The *diuturna emendatio* in this matter, instead of referring to the actual cessation of the infamy, may refer to the amount of time required for the amendment to become known to the people of the parish or the neighborhood, before such an admission to Communion may be made.

Regarding the satisfaction which must be made for the scandal caused, the law states specifically that it must be antecedent to the actual reception of the Eucharist.[74] Accordingly the promise of making satisfaction after the reception of Communion does not suffice.

It must be a public and extra-sacramental satisfaction; for this there suffices a public breaking with the past evil way of life, or a well-known abandonment of the occasion of sin. The Ritual, accordingly, instructs the confessor:

> The priest must take great pains to decide in which instances absolution should be given, denied, or deferred lest he absolve such as are indisposed for this benefit—persons, for example who give no indication of contrition, who refuse to put an end to hatred and enmity, to make restitution when they are able, to give up an approximate occasion of sin, or in any other way refuse to forsake their sins and amend their life. To this class belong also such persons as those who have given scandal, unless they make public satisfaction and remove the scandal.[75]

---

to the unique form: "Corpus Domini sit tibi ad probationem hodie."—C. 23, C. II, q. 5. cf. *supra*, p. 19.

[74] ". . . nisi . . . publico scandalo prius satisfecerint."—canon 855.

[75] *Rituale Romanum, Pauli V Pontificis Maximi iussu editum, Aliorumque Pontificum cura recognitum, atque auctoritate Pii Papae XI ad*

Even in cases of danger of death, some satisfaction for scandal is demanded in the Ritual:

> But if anyone who is in danger of death goes to confession, he must be absolved from all sins and censures, regardless of how they are reserved, for in this case every instance of reserved sin becomes void. Yet whenever possible, he should first make satisfaction, if any is required of him.[76]

While this refers to the sacrament of penance, the Ritual repeats the requirement of satisfaction for scandal in a provision referring explicitly to Holy Viaticum:

> Care is to be taken above all lest it [Holy Viaticum] be brought to the unworthy, whereby others could be scandalized, unless they first have confessed and have made the necessary reparation for scandal publicly given.[77]

It is for the priest who is the confessor and the administrator of Holy Viaticum to decide the extent of the obligation of the sick person, upon taking into consideration the condition of the penitent and the extent of the scandal occasioned by the sinful conduct.[78] A recommendation of Oesterle may be employed in cases where the sick persons are *"in periculo mortis,"* namely that the sinner extra-sacramentally declare in writing or vocally before the confessor and two witnesses that he has renounced his sinful and scandalous way of life, or, where it is sufficient or where it is

---

normam Codicis Iuris accomodatum (2. ed., Neo Eboraci: Benziger Bros., 1944), Tit. III, cap. 1, n. 23 (hereafter cited as *Rituale Romanum auctoritate Pii XI ad C.I.C. accommodatum*). Translation taken from Weller, *The Roman Ritual* (3 vols., Vol. I, *The Sacraments and Processions*, Milwaukee; Bruce, 1950), p. 309 (hereafter cited as Weller).

[76] *Rituale Romanum auctoritate Pii XI ad C.I.C. accommodatum*, Tit. III, cap 1, n. 24; Weller, p. 309.

[77] *Rituale Romanum auctoritate Pii XI ad C.I.C. accommodatum*, Tit. IV, cap. 4, n. 2; Weller, p. 263.

[78] Hannon, *Holy Viaticum*, The Catholic University of America Canon Law Studies, n. 314 (Washington, D. C.: The Catholic University of America Press, 1951), pp. 134-135.

necessary, the sinner may disavow his past before the confessor alone. Even in these cases it is to be done extra-sacramentally.[79]

Vermeersch-Creusen, Coronata, and Hannon say that *"in articulo mortis"* it suffices that the confessor obtain the permission of the dying penitent to inform the faithful that the sick person wished to make the proper satisfaction as far as it was possible, though it is always preferable that there be two witnesses for this declaration.[80] In case there is any doubt as to the sincerity of the dying person the confessor should resolve it in favor of this person. The spirit of the legislation of the Church which makes the last sacraments as available as possible to dying persons seems to favor such a presumption.[81]

Regarding the matter of bringing Holy Viaticum to a notoriously infamous person in a place well known to be used for immoral purposes, e.g., a brothel, Oesterle cites De Smet in favor of the view that It may be brought to a harlot in such a place: a) if it is absolutely impossible for the penitent to be moved to another place, for instance to a hospital; b) if it is impossible to purge the place; c) if the Blessed Sacrament is brought secretly.[82] A fourth obvious condition must be added, namely: d) if the danger of scandal is absent.

It is true that the Blessed Sacrament should not be brought to some indecent place.[83] It is also true, however, that the sacraments were instituted for the sake of needful people, and such a person as is here considered would be most needful of Our Lord in the Most Blessed Sacrament in the last hours of her life. If, therefore, the four conditions mentioned above are present, a priest

---

[79] Oesterle, "Casus ad Canonem 855 C.J.C.," *Perfice Munus,* XIV (1939), 748.

[80] Vermeersch-Creusen, *Epitome,* II, 117; Coronata, *De Sacramentis,* I, 294; Hannon, *Holy Viaticum,* pp. 134-135.

[81] Hannon, *loc. cit.*

[82] Oesterle, "Casus ad Canonem 855 C.J.C.," *Perfice Munus,* XIV (1939), 749, note 23.

[83] "Relative to the place proper for the administration of Holy Viaticum in particular, there is scarcely any restriction, provided the place be not repugnant to the holiness of the sacrament."—Hannon, *Holy Viaticum,* p. 164.

should bring Holy Viaticum to an infamous person even though she is living in or present in a place used for immoral purposes.

The assurance of a doctor or even that of others attending the dying person would suffice for the priest to feel certain about the impossibility of moving the dying person to another place.

A priest who is called upon to bring Holy Viaticum to someone in a house of ill fame will more likely avoid the danger of scandal if he is accompanied by a detective or a policeman. For the avoidance of scandal to those who do see the priest approach the house, the priest should let it be seen that he is carrying the Blessed Sacrament, e.g., by leaving open to view his stole and by maintaining the proper reverential demeanor.

The Blessed Sacrament may not be brought publicly to the sick who openly live in concubinage or in a notoriously invalid marriage, though Vermeersch-Creusen leave open the possibility that this may be done secretly.[84] The priest who is to bring Communion must judge what measure of likelihood there is that Communion can be brought secretly and without any danger of scandal. In the event that there is any doubt in the matter, he should not bring Communion to the sick people involved until he has consulted the ordinary, who is the proper judge in the matter of infamy and scandal in his territory. If the other party in the invalid and illicit union leaves the house of the sick person, then amendment and satisfaction for the scandal has already taken place, or has been begun at least, and Communion may be brought to the sick person.

If, however, for some reason the other party cannot leave the house of the sick person, for instance, if there is no one else to take care of the one who is sick, then Communion may not be brought to the house. An exceptional case would occur in the event that the party who is well could not for some reason leave the house of the one who is sick, and at the same time the reason for not being able to leave would be perfectly obvious and just as well known to the public as the invalidity or the unlawfulness of

---

[84] *Epitome*, II, 80.

the union itself. In such a case, Berardi stated, Viaticum could be brought to the sick person.[85] The fact that there is almost always present in such cases the danger of scandal makes these cases to be extremely rare. Whenever they do occur, however, the ordinary should be consulted.

A special problem arises in regard to those who are living in a notoriously invalid union, but who for some reason, e.g., because of children born of the union, have been given permission by the ordinary to continue to live together as brother and sister. May they receive Communion publicly? There is no question here of penance and amendment of life, since both of these factors have been dealt with in the course of obtaining the permission for cohabitation from the ordinary. Satisfaction for the scandal, however, must be made here as in every case, before the public reception of Holy Communion. The Sacred Congregation of the Council gave a decision in such a case on November 18, 1922.[86]

The case concerned a woman living in an incestuous union with her brother, which facts were known publicly. This woman presented herself for confession to a religious priest conducting a mission in the parish church. The confessor, without demanding that the penitent leave the man with whom she lived in view of their children's needed support, gave her absolution and permission to receive Holy Communion publicly in proof of her submission. Actually the couple were living continently at the time. When the pastor became aware of this admission to the sacraments, he notified the bishop of the place, who declared that the woman should be excluded from Holy Communion until she should separate from the man and thereby repair the scandal before Holy Communion was received, as canon 855 demanded. The religious, being dissatisfied with this decision, made an appeal through the Procurator General of his Order to the Sacred Congregation of

---

[85] *De Recidivis et Occasionariis Opusculum* (2 vols., Faventiae: Ex Typographia Novelli, 1873), II, 166-167.

[86] "Circa l'ammissione di pubblici concubinari alla S. Communione," *Il Monitore Ecclesiastico,* XXXV (1923), 237; *Archiv für katholiches Kirchenrecht,* CIII (1923), 162; Bouscaren, *Digest,* I, 408-409; Beste, p. 500.

the Council.[87] The Congregation's response upheld the ordinary's decision as based on canon 855, which demands satisfaction for scandal as well as penance and amendment of life before Holy Communion may be received.

The couple given permission to live together as brother and sister, for the same reason, may not receive Communion publicly in the place where they are known to be living in an invalid union. Nor is the scandal which is caused by permitting such people to approach the Communion rail easily alleviated by any public explanations, no matter what form they may take. On the contrary, further scandal is occasioned by such explanations. To the laity, the Church's marriage legislation seems most complicated, and the presentation to their minds of the possibility of people living together in sin for years and then being given permission to continue cohabitation may not serve to instruct them that the Church merely tolerates this arrangement in order to prevent a greater evil; rather, it may give them the impression that there is a certain laxity in the Church's law, and that preference is shown in certain cases. Accordingly, satisfaction for the scandal by means of a public declaration of the permission granted by the ordinary would probably injure the Church more than it would save the reputation of the parties involved.

Such couples as have obtained permission to live together as brother and sister may certainly receive Communion publicly in a church where they are not known, or where their status is not known, and it is not likely that it will become known in the future.

---

[87] The questions placed before the Congregation are recorded in *Il Monitore Ecclesiastico*:

I. Supposita emendatione et difficultate separationis, potestne Episcopus et debet hos fratres (concubinarios cum filiis) prohibere ne ad Communionem accedant, donec separentur, ut scandalum reparent; aut potius exigere debet scandali reparationem alio praedicto modo (publica menstrua communione per annum) quin separentur?

Et quantum negative ad primum partem, affirmative ad alteram:

II. Quid Missionarii facere possint et debeant in similibus casibus?—*loc. cit.*

The Sacred Congregation upheld the decision of the ordinary with the simple reply: "Standum iudicio Ordinarii."

They are not actually unworthy to receive Communion, but they are at the same time unable to make satisfaction for the scandal which their apparent unworthiness has caused in their own parish or community.

Several other cases involving satisfaction for scandal have some practical importance and merit treatment here.

1. Masons and other members of condemned secret societies who have been given permission to continue passive membership in such societies for some reason, e.g., in order to take advantage of insurance benefits of the groups, are obliged not to wear or display any symbols or emblems of the society. Before being permitted the reception of Communion they must surrender such masonic emblems and any books and papers pertaining to the condemned society to the absolving priest, who, Oesterle says, should forward them to the ordinary, or, if for any reason he cannot do so, should himself burn them.[88]

2. Catholic parties in mixed marriages who permit the non-Catholic education of their children, whatever the reasons may be, should not be permitted the reception of Holy Communion, until the situation has been righted, and satisfaction for scandal has been made.[89]

3. Those who are under notorious censures will undoubtedly be at the same time infamous in fact. Canon 855 explicitly excludes the excommunicated and the interdicted from the reception of Communion. If absolution from the censure is given in the external forum, then those who were once under censure cannot receive Communion until some satisfaction has been made for the scandal caused. The Code, accordingly, while granting some freedom in the external forum to one still apparently under censure though he has been absolved in the internal forum, leaves it in the superior's hands to demand proof, or at least some legitimate presumption, for the absolution, before the censure may be considered as not binding in the external forum.[90] Noldin-Schönegger and Bouscaren-Ellis require, besides the public knowledge that the one under

---

[88] "Casus ad Canonem 855 C.J.C.," *Perfice Munus,* XVII (1939), 748.

[89] Prümmer, *Manuale Theologiae Moralis,* III, 109.

[90] Canon 2251.

censure has gone to confession, some other satisfaction before the concession of the absolution from the censure may be presumed.[91]

Authors have deduced from canon 855 certain norms which pertain to the denial of Holy Communion to the unworthy in those cases wherein the requirements for bringing about the cessation of infamy of fact as they are presented in canon 855 have not been fulfilled. These norms are presented in the following numbers.

1. To the *public* sinner *publicly* requesting It, Communion is to be denied. The public request means that the request is made before those who know the person to be unworthy, whether they be many or few.

2. To the *public* sinner *occultly* requesting It, Communion is also to be denied. The person thought to be publicly unworthy though actually not unworthy may, however, receive Communion in a church other than that in which he is deemed infamous. The minister of the sacrament there, moreover, would be obliged not to deny him Communion, whether he thought him to be unworthy or not, because of the consequent loss of his reputation, to which the person has a right in this place where he is not known to be unworthy. If, however, the priest of the second and new church foresees that it will be only a short time before the person's unworthiness will be known in his church too, he should deny Communion to the one requesting It.[92]

3. To an *occult* sinner *occultly* requesting Communion, It is to be denied, unless it is only from the confessional that the unworthiness is known. An occult request is made before the minister of the sacrament alone or before others who do not have the use of

---

91 Noldin-Schönegger, *De Censuris* (34. ed., Oeniponte-Lipsiae: Pustet, 1940), p. 34; Bouscaren-Ellis, *Canon Law, A Text and Commentary* (Milwaukee, Wisc.: Bruce, 1946; reprint in 1948), p. 828 (hereafter cited as Bouscaren-Ellis).

92 "Si crimen petentis notum non est in loco, ubi petit sacramentum, hoc negandum est, ubi criminis notitia brevi etiam ad illum locum perventura est; potius enim irreverentia sacramenti et scandalum fidelium praecavendum est, quam modica diffamationis acceleratio; quodsi eo perventura non est aut solum post diuturnum tempus, sacramentum negandum non est. . . ."—Noldin-Schmitt, III, 33-34; Cappello, *De Sacramentis,* I, 57; Coronata, *De Sacramentis,* I, 50.

reason, as young children,[93] or before any people who will not perceive the priest refusing Communion to the one presenting himself to receive It.[94]

4. To an *occult* sinner *publicly* requesting It, Communion is not to be denied. An exception to the rule is had when an occult sinner is known to be requesting Communion out of contempt for the Blessed Sacrament and religion; in such a case, Communion is to be denied him.[95]

Article III. Infamy as an Impediment to Holy Orders

Through the sacrament of Holy Orders there is conferred upon the one ordained a character indelible and sublime, the mark of one solemnly dedicated to prayer and sacrifice, and for that reason a mark which sets him apart from and above the men from whose midst he is taken. "For every high priest taken from among men is appointed for men in the things pertaining to God, that he may offer gifts and sacrifices for sins."[96]

This teaching invokes from the faithful a spontaneous response of affection and respect for their priests. The law, too, does not neglect to point out the obligation of the faithful to show reverence toward the clergy.[97] At the same time the Church's law reminds priests of the strict obligation which they have, namely, to excel the laity in virtue and in a life of sanctity, whereby to deserve their respect.[98]

It is easily seen, then, why it is that the Church does not allow anyone who has already lost his good name to receive Holy Orders or to exercise the Orders he has received. The Code in listing the class of persons barred from Holy Orders by a simple impediment includes those ". . . qui infamia facti laborant, dum ipsa, iudicio Ordinarii, perdurat."[99]

The requirement of a good reputation is, as one would expect,

---

[93] Capello, *De Sacramentis,* I, 58.
[94] Coronata, *De Sacramentis,* I, 50.
[95] Coronata, *De Sacramentis,* I, 51; Cappello, *De Sacramentis,* I, 58.
[96] Hebrews, 5, 1.
[97] Canon 119.
[98] Canon 124.
[99] Canon 986, 7°.

a requirement which has existed from the very beginning of the Church. The Apostles instructed the disciples in their choice of the first deacons: "Therefore, brethren, select from among you seven men *of good reputation,* full of the Spirit and of wisdom, that we may put them in charge of this work."[100] In writing to Timothy, moreover, Paul was explicit in requiring a good name in candidates for Orders. Of those to be deacons, he said: "And let them first be tried and if found without reproach let them be allowed to serve."[101] One to be a bishop, moreover, ". . . *must have a good reputation* with those who are outside, that he may not fall into disgrace and into a snare of the devil."[102]

Since the public and solemn penance of the early Church indicated a grave crime and accordingly defamed one's character, the *poenitentes* were always impeded from ordination.[103]

It was at the time of the glossators that the term *infamia facti* became popularized, and they themselves pointed out how it impeded one from Holy Orders.[104]

After the Council of Trent, as the concept of *infamia facti* gradually but greatly broadened, a distinction was usually made between the reception of Orders and the exercise of Orders received, and more specifically between the acquisition of a benefice and the retention of a benefice already acquired.[105]

Before all detailed discussion regarding the effects of this impedi-

---

[100] Acts, 6, 3.

[101] I Tim., 3, 10.

[102] I Tim., 3, 7.

[103] *Supra,* pp. 10-13.

[104] *Glossa ord.* ad c. 16, X, *de purgatione canonica,* V, 34,—*ad verbum "postquam"*; et ad c. 3, D. LI,—*ad verbum "infamiae"*; cf. c. 14, *de purgatione canonica,* V, 34; c. 56, X, *de testibus et attestationibus,* II, 20; c. 8, D. LXXVII.

[105] Fermosinus, *Omnia Opera, Canonica, Civilia et Criminalia* (15 vols., Coloniae Allobrogum, 1741), XI, § 11, p. 24 (hereafter cited as Fermosinus). Concerning these distinctions it may be noted that even today the law provides that infamy of fact bars one from the licit acquisition of a benefice, according to canon 2294, § 2, but not necessarily from the retention of a benefice.—cf. *infra,* p. 123. The Code does, however, prohibit the infamous from the exercise of Orders (canons 968, § 2, and 2294, § 2), as well as from the reception of Orders (canon 986, 7°).—cf. *infra,* p. 130.

ment to Orders according to the present legislation, it is necessary to explain what the term "impediment" means.

A "simple impediment" is a canonical hindrance, temporary in nature, which of itself prohibits primarily the reception of Orders.[106]

It it called a *canonical* hindrance, not only to show the exclusive right of the Church to establish an obstacle to the reception of Orders, but also to separate it from the prohibitions which are based solely on the natural and positive divine law.[107]

An impediment is said to be *temporary* in nature, and thereby it is distinguished from an irregularity. An irregularity is a permanent hindrance to the reception of Orders and the exercise thereof, which hindrance is established by the Church's law.[108] The permanence of the irregularity marks the specific difference between it and a simple impediment. There are fourteen irregularities and seven impediments listed in the Code of Canon Law.[109]

Before the Code the terms "irregularity" and impediment" were used interchangeably. There were, however, always distinguishable among the irregularities certain ones which could be counteracted in the course of time and which are now designated with the term "impediment."[110]

Impediments as well as irregularities prevent the licit reception of Holy Orders and the exercise of the Orders already received. For the valid reception of Orders the law merely requires a validly baptized person of the male sex.[111]

Since infamy of fact is extant even before the ordinary's judgment, infamy and the impediment may be said to be present even before the ordinary declares that they are definitely present in a particular case.[112] Once the ordinary does judge that the infamy

[106] Vogelpohl, p. 3.

[107] Gasparri, *De Sacra Ordinatione,* I, 92; Cappello, *De Sacramentis,* IV, 330; Vogelpohl, p. 4.

[108] Canon 983; cf. Cappello, *De Sacramentis,* IV, 330.

[109] Canon 984 lists seven irregularities *ex defectu,* canon 985 seven irregularities *ex delicto,* canon 987 seven simple impediments.

[110] Vogelpohl, p. 3.

[111] Canon 968, § 1.

[112] Cf. *supra,* pp. 65-68.

has ceased, however, the impediment is at the same time judged to be non-extant. Impediments generally cease when their causes cease, and infamy of fact is the cause of the impediment considered here. Just as the impediment consequent upon military service ceases when one is mustered out of service, so the impediment effected by *infamia facti* ceases when one has regained his good reputation among the good and upright Catholics who previously thought ill of him. The judgment of the ordinary serves as a declaration of what to his mind is the real status of an individual in regard to his reputation among those who know him.

The impediment, strictly considered, does not *cease* when an infamous person moves to a place where he is unknown. In the place where his reputation is as yet unimpaired there is no infamy of fact and no impediment which could cease. If his acquaintances still think ill of him back in the place from which he moved, his status there is that of one infamous and impeded from Orders. The ordinary of the individual's new domicile may still refuse to ordain him in view of the crimes or reckless living which caused the infamy in the other locality, or of the possibility of the repetition of such misconduct, or of the danger that the evils known to others will become known to the people of the individual's new domicile.

The ordinary in judging that a person is not a suitable candidate for Orders, even though there be not present any canonical impediment, acts within his rights. By such a rejection he does not establish another "impediment."[113] It is true that the impediments are generally thought to be subject to a strict interpretation, but the ordinary is not restricted in his judgment as to those who are worthy of ordination and the exercise of Orders by the list of impediments in canon 987. Thus the Code says that one who has already received Orders is not to be prevented from the exercise of those Orders by the bishop unless there is present some canonical impediment or *some other grave cause.*[114]

---

[113] The possibility of establishing an impediment or an irregularity other than those which already are established by the Code is ruled out by canon 983.

[114] Canon 973, § 2.

Infamia facti cannot be removed by way of a dispensation,[115] and it would be unreasonable to suppose that the impediment arising from *infamia facti* could be removed on the basis of the provisions of the Code for a dispensation from impediments and irregularities.[116] If a person has a bad reputation in one place and a good reputation in another place, he does not need a dispensation in order to be ordained in that place where his reputation is unimpaired, simply because no impediment exists there. If an individual is irregular because of some crime listed in canon 985, and is at the same time infamous in fact, the dispensation from the irregularity does not necessarily effect a cessation of the impediment arising from *infamia facti,* which impediment is to be counteracted by the cessation of the infamy of fact, especially through a long period of amendment.

The Code in listing those who are infamous by reason of infamy of fact among the ones simply impeded from Holy Orders leaves open the possibility that such individuals will in time be able to receive Orders. Just how often it will happen that one who was once infamous, but who later regained his good reputation, will be considered an acceptable candidate for Orders it is difficult to estimate. Many feel with good reason that once an individual has been infamous, he may always be presumed unworthy of ordination.[117] The history of the Church, however, bears out the fact that a great number of those whom we consider our leading saints were converted from their infamous pasts to lives of extraordinary piety and sanctity. Those who find Christ after a careless way of life often serve Him best, as was the case with St. Paul, ". . . who before baptism was guilty of murder, yet afterwards was made an Apostle. . . ."[118]

---

[115] *Supra,* p. 75.

[116] Canons 990, 991.

[117] "But when one considers the very definition of infamy of fact (canon 2293, § 3), it seems that such a presumption of non-vocation would be rarely overcome."—Carr, *Vocation to the Priesthood: Its Canonical Concept,* The Catholic University of America Canon Law Studies, n. 293 (Washington, D. C.: The Catholic University of America Press, 1950), p. 70.

[118] *Glossa ord.* ad c. 3, D. XXVI, *ad verba "inter peccata."*

Canonically there is no impediment to Orders for an individual who has regained his good reputation, especially after a long period of amendment. The glossators noted, however, that such a person should not be consecrated a bishop because of a certain defect in his character.[119]

According to the Code, impediments bar one from the exercise of Orders received as well as from the reception of Orders (although the prohibition against the reception of Orders is the direct *primary* effect of an impediment, and the prohibition against the exercise of Orders already received is the *secondary* effect of an impediment).[120]

Cappello[121] and Regatillo,[122] in spite of the explicit statement of the Code, hold that impediments do not *ipso iure* carry with them a prohibition against the exercise of Orders received. Other authors, such as Blat,[123] Beste,[124] and Wernz-Vidal[125] do not admit this conclusion. At any rate, those who are impeded from Orders because of infamy of fact are explicitly hindered from the exercise of Orders by reason of canon 2294, § 2, whereby they are prevented from the exercise of the sacred ministry.[126]

Infamy of fact, however, is not an absolute impediment to the exercise of Orders, for a person is said to be infamous only in those places where he has lost his good reputation. A bishop, then, may feel that a cleric of his diocese who has become infamous in fact will the better rehabilitate himself and overcome the waywardness which led to his infamy, if he continues his priestly work

---

[119] *Loc. cit.* Under this view the glossators considered infamy of fact to be, in regard to the episcopate, a *permanent* impediment, which is called an "irregularity" in the Code today.

[120] Canon 968, § 2: "Qui irregularitate aliove impedimento detinentur, licet post ordinationem etiam sine propria culpa exorto, prohibentur receptos ordines exercere."

[121] *De Sacramentis,* IV, 339.

[122] *Ius Sacramentarium,* II, 83.

[123] *Commentarium,* Lib. III, Pars I, p. 437.

[124] *Introductio in Codicem,* p. 515.

[125] *Ius Canonicum,* IV, Pars I, 341.

[126] *Infra,* p. 131.

in another environment, namely in another assignment in his own diocese or in some other diocese where his reputation is still intact.

If the bishop feels that punishment is demanded in some case of a cleric who has become infamous, as would especially be true of a cleric who repeated the crimes which caused him to lose his good name previously, a period of penance in some religious atmosphere should be prescribed. Even when the priest has been reassigned, however, he should make manifest to the bishop his amendment of life, and should report to the bishop regularly, so that he may truly be said to be under the bishop's surveillance, as, in a very real sense, he would be in the place where he performs his penance.

If the penance prescribed within the judgment of the ordinary is not performed in or near the place wherein the cleric became infamous, the cleric should not be permitted to return to that place, and he should especially not be permitted to exercise the sacred ministry there.

As regards religious destined for the priesthood, it is to be noted that those who are debarred from Sacred Orders by some irregularity or canonical impediment are not licitly admitted to the novitiate.[127] Strictly taken, *infamia facti* would be included here. Furthermore, testimonial letters required for one applying for admittance into religious life must actually include information concerning his reputation.[128]

There is good reason, however, to believe that this impediment does not restrict one from licitly entering religion or the novitiate. The period of time which separates the admission and ordination is a long one and, although the novitiate is not designed as a penitential period as such, nevertheless it may serve as the period of amendment required by law for the cessation of *infamia facti.* Then, too, the admission and the novitiate can be effected in a

---

[127] "Illicite, sed valide admittuntur . . . ad sacerdotium in religione destinati, a quo tamen removeantur irregularitate aliove canonico impedimento. . . ."—canon 542, 2°.

[128] Canon 545, § 4.

place which is far enough away from the place in which the infamy exists to make remote any danger of scandal.[129]

This does not mean, of course, that persons of ill-repute may be admitted to the religious life indiscriminately. Only those who manifest a sincere conversion to and an ardent love of God should be so admitted. This is required by the Holy See, in the words of Pope Pius IX as quoted in an Instruction of the Sacred Congregation of Religious:

> Since the welfare and the honor of every religious family depends entirely on the careful selection of novices and their excellent training, We most earnestly exhort you to investigate diligently beforehand the dispositions, character and morality of those who are to become members of your institute. . . .[130]

The investigation prescribed by law previous to ordination regularly precludes the danger that a person infamous by infamy of fact in any degree will be ordained. It is the pastor of the parish in which the individual has his domicile who will be most helpful in providing information as to the candidate's reputation in the parish. This refers not only to his reputation as a Catholic, but also to his reputation as a candidate for Orders. The pastor must answer to "what is the public opinion regarding his vocation?" in the form of investigation which he must forward to the ordinary before the individual may be tonsured or ordained.[131]

If for some reason the pastor is not well acquainted with the attitude of the parishioners towards the candidate, this should be made known to him as a result of the banns which must be publicly announced or posted in the parish church.[132]

---

[129] Aldeaseca, *De Admissione Novitiorum,* Dissertatio ad Lauream in Facultate Iuris Canonici Pontificiae Universitatis Gregorianae (Vallisoleti: Typis Sever-Cuesta, 1951), p. 95.

[130] Pius IX, allocut. *Ubi primum,* 17 iun. 1847—*Fontes,* n. 506; S. C. de Religiosis, 1 dec. 1931, n. 4—*AAS,* XXIV (1932), 75.

[131] S. C. de Sacramentis, instr. 27 dec. 1930, Forma II, n. 15—*AAS,* XXIII (1930), 128.

[132] Canon 998.

Then, too, the testimonial letters required by the Code before a candidate may be ordained serve to inform the bishop of ordination of the reputation of the ordinand. This is especially true of those letters which are required of the local ordinaries in whose territory the candidate has dwelt for the length of time required to contract any of the canonical impediments.[133] Generally the duration of time in which the law considers that a canonical impediment may have been incurred is three months for those who were in military service, and six months for others. It is such periods of time as have lapsed after one has reached the age of puberty that are the law's concern here.[134]

It may happen that a bishop who is asked to give testimonial letters certifying the absence of impediments to Orders in some individual judges that, although there is not present the canonical impediment that arises from *infamia facti,* there is something in the candidate's life or morals, as evidenced during the time spent in the bishop's diocese, which does render the candidate unfit for the priesthood. In such a case the bishop should make this known to the bishop who asked for the information. It may be done either in the testimonial letter itself, or in a separate private letter.[135]

---

[133] Canon 993, 4°.

[134] Canon 994, § 1.

[135] Cappello, *De Sacramentis,* IV, 398; Quinn, *Documents Required for the Reception of Orders,* The Catholic University of America Canon Law Studies, n. 266 (Washington, D. C.: The Catholic University of America Press, 1948), p. 107.

CHAPTER V

THE EFFECTS OF INFAMY OF FACT AS REGARDS NON-SACRAMENTAL MATTERS

The Church is the Mystical Body of Christ, and its members who hold the positions of dignity and possess the privileges of the Church must command the respect which befits such positions. By prohibiting those who are infamous from occupying honorable positions and from possessing privileges, the Church not only punishes individuals for whatever evil deeds may have brought about their infamy, but it also preserves free from disgrace the excellent positions and functions it bestows. While many of the subjects of this chapter may not be totally distinct from the subject of the administration of the sacraments, which was dealt with in the foregoing chapter, these subjects do allow of the independent treatment which here is given them. This present chapter deals principally with the effects of infamy as presented in canon 2294 of the Code of Canon Law, and likewise as involved in the evaluating of the testimony of infamous witnesses.

Article I. The Comparison between the Effects of Infamy of Law and of Infamy of Fact as Listed in Canon 2294

It is canon 2294 which presents the most complete listing of the effects of *infamia iuris* and *infamia facti*:

> § 1. *Qui infamia iuris laborat, non solum est irregularis ad normam can.* 984, *n.* 5, *sed insuper est inhabilis ad obtinenda beneficia, pensiones, officia et dignitates ecclesiasticas, ad actus legitimos perficiendos, ad exercitium iuris aut muneris ecclesiastici, et tandem arceri debet a ministerio in sacris functionibus exercendo.*
>
> § 2. *Qui laborat infamia facti, repelli debet tum a recipiendis ordinibus ad normam can.* 987, *n.* 7, *dignitatibus, beneficiis, officiis ecclesiasticis, tum ab exercendo sacro ministerio et ab actibus legitimis ecclesiasticis.*

There is but a slight variation in the two listings of the effects of infamy. It is stated that those who are infamous by infamy of law cannot obtain *pensions,* or exercise ecclesiastical *rights* and *functions* (*munera*), whereas these particular effects are not predicated for those who are infamous by infamy of fact. The two lists are otherwise similar to each other as regards the subjects which they contain.

The one important distinction, however, lies in the fact that, whereas those who are infamous by infamy of law are incapable of *validly* holding positions, and of exercising the privileges mentioned, those who are infamous by infamy of fact cannot *licitly* hold these same positions or exercise such rights.[1] Persons infamous by infamy of law accordingly cannot validly obtain ecclesiastical benefices, pensions, offices and dignities, nor can they validly perform legally authorized ecclesiastical acts, nor can they validly exercise ecclesiastical rights or functions.

An exception is made in the canon in regard to the functions of the sacred ministry, e.g., the administration of the sacraments, which cannot be rendered invalid. The law calls upon superiors to see to it that those who are infamous by infamy of law are prevented from exercising the sacred functions of the ministry ("... arceri debet a ministerio in sacris functionibus exercendo"). Whereas the other functions are performed *invalidly* by those who are infamous by infamy of law, the functions of the sacred ministry are performed *illicitly* by these same individuals.

Infamy of fact has no invalidating effects at all. Whatever function one infamous by infamy of fact performs, he performs validly, but if it be one of those functions as are mentioned in canon 2294, he performs it illicitly.

Both infamy of law and infamy of fact make illicit the reception of Holy Orders, infamy of law being an irregularity, infamy of fact an impediment. In stating this fact, canon 2294 repeats the provisions of earlier canons.[2] Concerning those who are infamous by infamy of fact, as has been noted, no mention is made of an

---

[1] Berutti, *De Delictis,* p. 226; Cocchi, *Commentarium,* VIII, 193; Gasparri, *De Sacra Ordinatione,* I, 199.

[2] Canons 984, 5°, 987, 7°; cf. *supra,* pp. 110-118.

exclusion from the reception of pensions and the exercise of functions (*munera*), though the exclusion from such pensions and functions is predicated for those who are infamous by infamy of law. It cannot be asserted that personal pensions are included under the notion of benefices, for the Code indicates that personal pensions, while similar in nature to benefices, do not come under the term "benefice" in the law.[3]

The law does not bar those who are infamous by infamy of fact from enjoying ecclesiastical rights and performing ecclesiastical functions (*"iura et munera"*), though it states that those who are infamous by infamy of law cannot validly exercise them. The prohibition of the licit exercise of certain rights and functions, however, is contained in the other restrictions placed on the infamous by infamy of fact in canon 2294, § 2.

"Munera" denote in a general way functions with all their attendant rights and obligations.[4] Ecclesiastical functions, moreover, are directed towards a spiritual end, namely the glory of God and the salvation of souls, and are to be identified with ecclesiastical offices

---

[3] "Licite aliquam cum beneficiis similitudinem praeseferant, in iure tamen beneficii nomine non veniunt . . . pensiones personales."—canon 1412, 4°. A pension is a source of income derived from a benefice not one's own, and may be obtained by a cleric, as canon 118 states. The term "pension" allows of a distinction between the so-called *pensio in titulum beneficii,* and the *pensio in stipendium.*—Gass, *Ecclesiastical Pensions,* The Catholic University of America Canon Law Studies, n. 157 (Washington, D. C.: The Catholic University of America Press, 1942), pp. 5-8. The *pensio in titulum beneficii* can obtain when a church enjoys an abundant revenue but is without a regular minister. The legitimate authority can in such a case designate it as a perpetual benefice, e.g., a perpetual vicarship, for a cleric to whom is to be assigned a portion of the fruits of that church as an annual income. Such a pension, Gass says, amounts to a benefice for all practical purposes, and is but improperly called a pension.—*op. cit.,* p. 8. It is the *pensio in stipendium,* the pension properly so-called, which is here excluded from the notion of benefice. A pronouncement of the Sacred Congregation of the Council in the last century pointed out the clear distinction between pensions and benefices. Cf. S.C.C., *Ventimilien.,* 17 dec. 1836—*Fontes,* n. 4061.

[4] "Munus, i.e. cumulus iurium et obligationum. . . ."—Coronata, *Institutiones,* I, 239.

in the broad sense: "Officium ecclesiasticum lato sensu est quodlibet munus quod in spiritualem finem legitime exercetur. . . ."[5]

It is not, however, because of the term *"officium"* in canon 294, § 2, that those who are infamous by infamy of fact are to be excluded from ecclesiastical functions, since *"officium"* in the Code must be understood in the strict sense.[6] It is principally because of the prohibition that is placed on those who are infamous by infamy of fact in regard to the authorized ecclesiastical acts[7] that those who are infamous can be said to be excluded from ecclesiastical functions. The more important functions (e.g., the administration of church property) and rights (e.g., of voting and of patronage) are included in the notion of authorized ecclesiastical acts.

What of the other less important ecclesiastical functions of the clergy and religious as well as those of the laity, such as the functions performed by choirmembers, Mass-servers, organists, janitors, sacristans, etc.?[8] There is certainly no provision in the law whereby persons infamous by infamy of fact are forbidden the performance of these functions. The lawgiver, moreover, has omitted all mention of such a prohibition in spite of the explicit denial of the right to perform such functions to those who are infamous by infamy of law. Nevertheless, the moral law would dictate that administrators prohibit persons of ill-repute from performing functions which pertain to the glory of God and the salvation of souls, by reason of the danger of scandal. Gasparri accordingly taught quite explicitly that infamy of fact does exclude one from public functions.[9]

---

[5] Canon 145, § 1; cf. Abbo-Hannan, I, 208; McBride, *Incardination and Excardination of Seculars,* The Catholic University of America Canon Law Studies, n. 145 (Washington, D. C.: The Catholic University of America Press, 1941), p. 428 (hereafter cited as McBride).

[6] This is true unless the context in which the term appears clearly allows of an interpretation of "office" in the broad sense (which exception is not verified in canon 2294, § 2). This provision is contained in canon 145, § 2.

[7] Canon 2256, § 2.

[8] Coronata, *Institutiones,* II, 239; Beste, p. 199; Augustine, VIII, 245.

[9] *De Sacra Ordinatione,* I, 199.

Article II. Infamy of Fact and the Reception of Dignities, Benefices and Offices

"Qui laborat infamia facti, repelli debet a recipiendis . . . dignitatibus, beneficiis, officiis. . . ."—canon 2294, § 2.

The law states that those who are infamous by infamy of fact are to be refused the *reception* of ecclesiastical dignities, benefices and offices. Just as, however, before the Code a distinction was made between the acquisition of and the retention of a benefice,[10] so, too, canon 2294, § 2, by way of an implicit distinction, does not demand that those who are infamous are to be refused the *retention* of the dignities, benefices or offices which they have received. The law recognizes a certain *ius quaesitum* on the part of a dignitary, beneficiary or office-holder, and does not require that the ordinary deprive them of their dignity, office or benefice. It is certain, therefore, that the deprivation of an office, etc., is not provided for in the canon here under discussion. It is true even of the penalty of infamy of law, and of any disabling law, that the *iura quaesita* are not lost when there is lost the right to exercise the functions associated with them, unless the penalty of deprivation is joined with the disabling law in a particular case.[11]

It cannot be denied, however, that the ordinary may judge that the infamy is a reason for removing one from an office or a bene-

---

[10] Molina, *De Iustitia et Iure* (3 vols. in 4, Coloniae Allobrogum, 1759), Lib. IV, tract. IV, disc. 11, n. 3; *Decisiones Recensiores*, pars 19, tome 2, decis. 501, nn. 3, 4, p. 249. The Rota here distinguished between the privation of and the acquisition of a benefice, insisting that infamy of law in connection either with a condemnatory or a declaratory sentence was required to warrant the deprivation of a benefice. Infamy of fact, however, and *"diffamatio,"* through which one's reputation was ruined among prudent men, sufficed for preventing the acquisition of a benefice.

[11] Canon 2296, § 1. Instances of *latae sententiae* deprivation are to be found in canons 2396; 2397; 2398; 2266. Cases of *ferendae sententiae* deprivation are mentioned in canons 2314, § 1, 2°; 2331, § 2; 2343, § 2, 3°; 2345; 2350, § 2; 2354, § 2; 2359, §§ 1-3; 2368, § 1; 2381, 2°; 2180 and 2181 together with 2177. There are still other cases wherein it is left to the judgment of the ordinary whether or not to deprive one of a benefice or office by way of punishment, as illustrated in canons 2324; 2336, § 1; 2355; 2360, § 2; 2359, § 2; 2394, 2°; 2403; 2305.

fice. The law deals not only with an *ipso iure* deprivation of office, but also with one that remains to be inflicted through the action of the proper superior.[12] If the office is a revocable office or benefice, any just cause suffices for the removal of the beneficiary or office-holder.[13] For an irrevocable office or benefice, the norms of law as enacted in canons 2147-2156 are to be followed in the matter of the removal of the beneficiary or office-holder.[14] These norms in canons 2147-2156 include among the reasons for the removal of an irremovable pastor the loss of his good reputation,[15] which, if it is not the same as infamy of fact, is even less serious and less harmful than infamy itself, which is brought about by the commission of a delict or a depraved way of life. Infamy of fact is, then, reason enough for the removal of an irremovable pastor and, *a fortiori,* the removal of a removable pastor.[16]

The inherent reason for the removal of an infamous person from an office, etc., is the same as the prohibition against admitting them to offices, etc., in the first place, namely the danger of grave scandal, and the fact that one cannot faithfully and effectively fulfill the divine ministry when one has lost the respect of the people.[17]

Dignities, offices and benefices will best be considered independently.

Section 1. The Nature of Dignities

"Dignitates" in the Code has at times a highly technical meaning and in other contexts a less technical meaning. The *"dignitates"* or dignitaries, strictly so-called, together with the canons are the two groups which constitute cathedral and collegiate chapters.[18] The dignitaries are distinguished from the canons and the other members of the chapter by reason of their offices, which offices

---

[12] Canon 192, § 1.

[13] ". . . qualibet iusta causa. . . ."—canon 192, § 3: ". . . ob alias rationabiles causas. . . ."—canon 2299, § 1.

[14] Canon 192, § 2.

[15] Canon 2147, § 1, 3°. Cf. *supra,* pp. 57-58.

[16] Canon 2157, § 1: "Parochus quoque amovibilis a sua paroecia amoveri potest ex iusta et gravi causa ad normam can. 2147."

[17] Beste, p. 880.

[18] Canon 393, § 1.

contain some powers of jurisdiction not common to other members of the chapter.[19]

The interpretation of the expression "ecclesiastical dignities," however, need not be taken in the strict sense, nor need it be controlled by the rules governing chapters. This exception holds true in the United States, where the cathedral chapters are replaced by boards of diocesan consultors.[20] The principle implied in the word "dignity" does obtain, however, and the note of some added dignity is applicable according to the less technical understanding of the word to: 1) the diocesan consultors;[21] 2) members of the Pontifical household;[22] 3) diocesan officials, such as the *officialis,* the synodal and pro-synodal judges, the synodal and pro-synodal examiners, etc., 4) possessors of ecclesiastical degrees of the doctorate or the licentiate.[23]

Those who have become infamous by infamy of fact may not licitly obtain these dignities.

Section 2. The Nature of Offices

An office in the broad sense is any function which is exercised according to the norms of the law for the glory of God and the good of souls.[24] The incumbent of an office in the broad sense may be a lay person, since there is no power of jurisdiction or of Orders necessarily involved in such an office.

The term "ecclesiastical office," however, is to be taken in the strict sense unless the contrary is apparent in a particular canon.[25] This ecclesiastical office, strictly so-called, is a function perma-

---

19 Cf. canon 393, § 1; Woywod, *A Practical Commentary,* I, 140; Vermeersch-Creusen, *Epitome,* I, 367; Coronata, *Institutiones,* I, 515; Eagleton, *The Diocesan Quinquennial Faculties, Formula IV,* The Catholic University of America Canon Law Studies, n. 248 (Washington, D. C.: The Catholic University of America Press, 1948), p. 126 (hereafter cited as Eagleton).

20 Eagleton, p. 127.

21 Canons 423-428.

22 Canon 328. Cf. Gasparri, *De Sacra Ordinatione,* II, 192; Sole, *De Delictis et Poenis,* p. 196; Moretti, *De Sacris Functionibus* (4 vols., Taurini: Marietti, 1936-1939), I, 59.

23 Cf. canons 1377-1378.

24 Canon 145, § 1. Cf. *supra,* pp. 121-122.

25 Canon 145, § 2.

nently established by divine law or ecclesiastical ordinance conferred according to the rules of canon law, carrying with it some participation in ecclesiastical power either of Orders or of jurisdiction.[26]

There are four specific elements in the definition of an office in the strict sense.

1) It must be *permanently established,* which is to say that the office itself and not the incumbent's tenure of office is permanent.[27]

2) It must be *established by divine law or ecclesiastical ordinance.* Some offices, such as the papacy and the episcopate, are of divine institution; others, such as that of the metropolitan, the vicar-general, the pastor, are of ecclesiastical origin.[28]

3) It must be *conferred according to the rules of canon law.* The norms which the Code provides for the conferring of offices are contained in canons 147-182.

4) It must carry with it *some participation in the power of Orders or of jurisdiction.* If the power is that of jurisdiction, it must be ordinary, that is, a power attached by the law itself to the office.[29] The majority of the authors take this for granted.[30] Sipos,[31]

---

[26] Canon 145, § 1.

[27] Blat, Lib. II, p. 112; Vermeersch-Creusen, *Epitome,* I, 243; Bouscaren-Ellis, p. 122; McBride, pp. 430-431; McDevitt, *The Renunciation of an Ecclesiastical Office,* The Catholic University of America Canon Law Studies, n. 218 (Washington, D. C.: The Catholic University of America Press, 1946), p. 3 (hereafter cited as McDevitt).

[28] Maroto distinguishes between the institution of an office *in genere* and its institution *in specie.* Thus Christ established the episcopate as an office for the Church universal; this is the constitution of the office *in genere.* The Roman Pontiff determines the bishoprics; this is the constitution of the offices *in specie.-Institutiones Iuris Canonici* (2 vols., Vol. I, 3. ed., 1921, Vol. II, 1919, Romae: Apud Commentarium pro Religiosis), I, 678-679 (hereafter cited as Maroto).

[29] Canon 197, § 1: "Potestas iurisdictionis ordinaria ea est quae ipso iure adnexa est officio."

[30] Wernz-Vidal, *Ius Canonicum,* II, 195; Maroto, I, 676; Coronata, *Institutiones,* I, 332-333; Bouscaren-Ellis, p. 122; McDevitt, pp. 5-6; Manning, *The Free Conferral of Offices,* The Catholic University of America Canon Law Studies, n. 219 (Washington, D. C.: The Catholic University of America Press, 1945), p. 23; Hilling, "Kirchliches Officium und Potestas Ordinaria," *Archiv für katholisches Kirchenrecht* (Innsbruck, 1857-1861, Mainz, 1862-), CXVII (1937), 433.

[31] *Enchiridion Iuris Canonici,* p. 127.

McBride,[32] and Vermeersch-Creusen,[33] however, maintain that an office may be had also if merely delegated power be attached to it. Sipos claims that the definition of ordinary power in canon 197, § 1, as the power which is attached by the law itself to an office, does not warrant the conclusion that every office must have ordinary power. Thus, the delegated power which is attached to the position of synodal judge by the superior's appointment would be sufficient to constitute it an office in the strict sense.

Hilling maintains that, although the definition itself of an office does not make it clear that "office" and "ordinary power" are correlative terms, the comparison of the definition of an office with the definition of ordinary power does make this point clear. Ordinary power is that power which is inherent in the office; delegated power is complementary to the office. According to this reasoning, then, synodal judges, since they have merely delegated power, do not have an office in the strict sense.

There is also a dispute in regard to the power of Orders required for the constitution of an office in the strict sense. Vidal (1867-1938)[34] and Bouscaren-Ellis[35] maintain that the power of Orders attached to an office must be distinct from that which is conferred by ordination, because what is now required is a power attached to the office as such. Cocchi,[36] Claeys Bouuaert-Simenon,[37] McBride,[38] and Lynch[39] require no more than the power of Orders received at the time of ordination for a verification of the definition of an office in the strict sense.

---

[32] *Incardination and Excardination of Seculars,* pp. 445-448.

[33] *Epitome,* II, n. 742.

[34] *Ius Canonicum,* II, 194.

[35] *Canon Law, A Commentary,* p. 122.

[36] *Commentarium,* II, n. 59, p. 147.

[37] *Manuale Juris Canonici,* I, n. 306, p. 189.

[38] *Incardination and Excardination of Seculars,* p. 437.

[39] *Coadjutors and Auxiliaries of Bishops,* The Catholic University of America Canon Law Studies, n. 238 (Washington, D. C.: The Catholic University of America Press, 1947), p. 42 (hereafter cited as Lynch).

These controversies would indeed allow of greater discussion than is apropos of the question of infamy of fact. Those positions, however, concerning which there is a doubt whether or not they are ecclesiastical offices in the strict sense of the word, e.g., the position of synodal judges, will certainly come under the heading of dignities, from which the infamous are also barred. This is true also of the controversy concerning the connotation of the term "jurisdiction" in regard to the position of diocesan chancellor.[40] Such a position is, if not an office, a dignity from which the infamous are barred.[41]

Offices as mentioned in the Code of Canon Law are held by the following persons: The Roman Pontiff, residential bishops,[42]

---

[40] McBride points out that the position of chancellor ". . . does not have included in itself any participation whatsoever in the power of orders or of jurisdiction, either by the law itself, or by order of the law." He therefore concludes that the chancellor does not hold an ecclesiastical office in the strict sense.—*op. cit.,* p. 463. This is contrary to the position of Prince, *The Diocesan Chancellor,* The Catholic University of America Canon Law Studies, n. 167 (Washington, D. C.: The Catholic University of America Press, 1942), pp. 44-47 (hereafter cited as Prince); among other authors who hold the same opinion as Prince are to be included: Coronata, *Institutiones,* I, 504; Maroto, *Institutiones,* II, 15; Abbo-Hannan, I, 390; Manning, pp. 24-25. All of these authors classify chancellors among those who hold offices in the strict sense because of the chancellor's inherent share in the power of jurisdiction as it is exercised administratively.

[41] It is expressly stated in law, moreover, that the chancellor and all of the notaries must be persons of good reputation, *"integrae famae."* —canon 373, § 4. Likewise, the functions of the chancellor and the notaries constitute legally authorized ecclesiastical acts (canon 2256, § 2), which the infamous are not permitted to perform, according to canon 2294, § 2. Cf. *infra,* pp. 134-135.

[42] Canon 334, § 1. Those who hold that the power of Orders itself suffices for the holding of an office in the strict sense (cf. *supra,* p. 127), and who do not demand the ordinary power of jurisdiction inherent in the office itself (cf. *supra,* pp. 126-127)), conclude that the Coadjutors and Auxiliary Bishops mentioned in canons 350-355 hold an office in the strict sense of the word, and that this is the proper understanding of the use of the word "office" as used in canon 353, § 1.—Lynch, p. 42. By demanding for an office the inherent power of Orders or of jurisdiction, one may admit as office-holders only the *Coadiutor sedi datus* of canon 352 and the Auxiliary Bishop appointed to a bishop who is unable to administer his own office.

metropolitans,[43] abbots and prelates *nullius,*[44] vicars general,[45] apostolic administrators,[46] vicars and prefects apostolic,[47] vicars capitular,[48] major superiors of exempt cleris,[49] diocesan *officiales,*[50] *vice-officiales,*[51] canons of collegiate and cathedral chapters,[52] diocesan consultors,[53] vicars forane,[54] pastors,[55] rectors of churches,[56] rectors of seminaries,[57] parish vicars,[58] parish administrators,[59] substitute vicars,[60] parochial adjutants who are assigned to take the place of the pastor in all things, with the exception of the *Missa pro populo.*[61]

Section 3. The Nature of Benefices

The Code defines an ecclesiastical benefice in these terms:

> *Beneficium ecclesiasticum est ens iuridicum a competente ecclesiastica auctoritate in perpetuum constitutum seu erectum, constans officio sacro et iure percipiendi reditus ex dote officio adnexos.*[62]

---

[43] Canon 274.

[44] Canons 198, § 1, 323, § 1.

[45] Canons 198, § 1, 366, § 1.

[46] Canons 198, § 1, 315.

[47] Canons 198, § 1; 294.

[48] Canons 429-444. In the absence of a cathedral chapter the office of these vicars is filled by the diocesan administrators in the United States of America.

[49] Canons 198, §§ 1 and 2, 501, § 1.

[50] Canon 1573, § 1.

[51] Canons 1573, §§ 4 and 5, 1577, § 2, 1578.

[52] Canons 391-422.

[53] Canon 427.

[54] Canon 447.

[55] Canons 451-470.

[56] Canon 485.

[57] Canon 1368.

[58] The *vicarii actuales* of canon 471.

[59] The *vicarii oeconomi* of canons 472-473.

[60] The *vicarii substituti* of canon 474.

[61] Canon 475, § 2; cf. Bastnagel, *The Appointment of Parochial Adjutants and Assistants,* The Catholic University of America Canon Law Studies, n. 58 (Washington, D. C.: The Catholic University of America, 1930), p. 145.

[62] Canon 1409.

Five essential elements are contained in this definition.

1) A benefice is a *juridical entity,* that is a moral person, which by a fiction of law is some group or thing considered as the subject of rights and obligations.[63] A benefice is a non-collegiate moral person (as distinguished from a collegiate moral person which is composed of at least three physical persons).[64] The benefice is composed not of physical persons, but rather of a sacred office and the right to the revenue attached to the office.[65]

2) A benefice is *constituted or established by a competent ecclesiastical authority.* This establishment is to be accomplished by means of a legal document in which the location of the benefice is stated, and the endowment and the rights and obligations of the beneficiary are described.[66]

3) An ecclesiastical benefice is to be *permanently* established. It is because the benefice involves an office that it has this note of perpetuity.

4) A benefice must contain a *sacred office.* Every benefice is actually an ecclesiastical office in the strict sense, and is related to office as species to genus. The importance of the sacred office as a foundation of the benefice has always been stressed by theologians.[67]

5) A benefice carries with it the *right to receive from the endowment the revenue* attached to the office. The Code rules that the endowment of the benefice may be formed: a) by property owned by the moral person; b) by definite payments required of some family or moral person; c) by assured voluntary contributions of the faithful; d) by stole fees within the limitations constituted by diocesan statutes or legitimate custom; or e) by the distributions in connection with the duty of choir in collegiate

---

[63] Canon 99.

[64] Canon 100, § 2.

[65] Haydt, *Reserved Benefices,* The Catholic University of America Canon Law Studies, n. 161 (Washington, D. C.: The Catholic University of America Press, 1942), p. 62 (hereafter cited as Haydt).

[66] Canon 1418.

[67] Haydt, p. 65.

churches, exclusive of one-third of these distributions, if the only revenue of the benefice comes from such distributions.[68]

In the United States, ecclesiastical benefices are exemplified in the dioceses and in the parishes having a resident pastor, endowment (resources or revenue according to the provisions of canons 1410 or 1415, § 3), and boundaries.[69]

Article III. Infamy of Fact and the Exercise of the Sacred Ministry and of Authorized Ecclesiastical Acts

"Qui laborat infamia facti, repelli debet ad exercendo sacro ministerio et ab actibus legitimis ecclesiasticis."—canon 2294, § 2.

Section 1. The Exercise of the Sacred Ministry

Those who are infamous by infamy of fact are to be prohibited from exercising the sacred ministry. The sacred ministry pertains not merely to officials and beneficiaries, but also to all clerics in the exercise of their Orders. It includes the offering of Mass, the administration of the sacraments in general, and all other spiritual ecclesiastical functions, as the exposition of and benediction given with the Blessed Sacrament, preaching, the conducting of devotions, services and processions, the conferral of blessings and the performance of funeral services.

This prohibition repeats the prohibition to exercise Sacred Orders that is placed on those who incur an impediment such as *infamia facti* after ordination.[70]

Section 2. The Exercise of Authorized Ecclesiastical Acts

When it is said that those who are infamous are to be prevented from performing legally authorized acts, it is the acts enumerated in canon 2256, 2°, that are signified:

---

[68] Canon 1410.

[69] Private letter of the Apostolic Delegate to the United States addressed to the Bishops of the United States, Nov. 10, 1922.—Bouscaren, *Digest*, I, 149-151.

[70] Canons 968, § 2; 987, 7°. Cf. *supra*, p. 115.

Nomine autem actuum legitimorum ecclesiasticorum significantur: munus administratoris gerere bonorum ecclesiasticorum, partes agere iudicis, auditoris et relatoris, defensoris vinculi, promotoris iustitiae et fidei, notarii et cancellarii, cursoris et apparitoris, advocati et procuratoris in causis ecclesiastics, munus patrini agere in sacramentis baptismi et confirmationis, sufffragium ferre in electionibus ecclesiasticis, ius patronatus exercere.

This list stands all-inclusive.[71]

A. The Administration of Church Property

The administration of church property, Bouscaren-Ellis point out, may be compared to the government of persons. Government has as its purpose the preservation of the well-being of persons in order to help them to their proper end in life, and the administration of property has as its purpose the preservation of all temporal things which have been acquired and the use of them for their destined end.[72] The administration of ecclesiastical property is a privilege as well as a charge, and should be entrusted to men who deserve and who actually possess a good reputation. Furthermore, were the Church to allow men of bad reputation to administer its property, the faithful would find it difficult to respect or trust the Church in its dealing with spiritual matters as well as in its handling of temporal matters.

The Roman Pontiff is the supreme administrator and manager of all Church property.[73] The local ordinary is the guardian of diocesan property.[74] To help him in this guardianship, the ordinary must establish what is known as the diocesan council of administration, which consists of two or more capable men, skilled in canon and civil law, as far as this is possible. The ordinary chooses the members of this council after seeking the advice of his chapter (diocesan board of consultors), unless their appointment has

[71] Coronata, *Institutiones,* IV, 197; Augustine, VIII, p. 168, note 10.

[72] *Canon Law, A Commentary,* p. 764.

[73] Canon 1518.

[74] Canon 1519, § 1.

already been provided for in some other equivalent manner by particular law or custom.[75]

Besides this diocesan board of administration, the local ordinary must also appoint for three-year periods some prudent and capable men of good reputation (". . . *boni testimonii.* . . .") to serve as the local board of administration for the property of any church or pious place for which the law or the articles of foundation have provided no administrator.[76] Laymen are not excluded here, though usually clerics are appointed when the need for this board exists. Such a need will exist in certain financial foundations, but will only rarely be verified in parishes in the United States.

In many other countreis, however, it is customary for the ordinary to establish a parochial board of clerics and laymen, the *consilium fabricae* of canons 1183-1184, who join with the administrator of the parish in the administration of the parish property.[77] The parish trustees or councilmen in the United States, although they have much less authority and power than the *consilium fabricae,* have duties enough to warrant their classification among the administrators of church property mentioned in canon 2256, 2°.

Besides the administrators of parochial properties, there are included the administrators of the properties of Third Orders, pious unions and confraternities lawfully established according to canons 100 and 687, the directors of hospitals, of orphan asylums and of other such institutions established by the ordinary.[78]

The ordinary may remove any of these administrators from their posts, if their infamy is sufficiently serious to warrant such removal.

---

[75] Canon 1520, § 1. In many dioceses of the United States the ordinary provides that the diocesan board of consultors (cf. canons 423-428) serve also as the board of administration. The ordinary, however, may appoint laymen to the board of administration, whereas laymen cannot serve on the diocesan board of consultors. For the functions of the board of administration, see canons 1415, § 2; 1532; 1539, § 2; 1541; § 2; 1653, § 1.

[76] Canon 1521, § 1.

[77] They are distinguished from the aforementioned local board of administration in this that the board of administration administers church property when no administrator is otherwise provided either in law or in the articles of foundation.

[78] Canon 1489.

B. Taking Part in Ecclesiastical Trials

It is most reasonable that those who take part in the Church's administration of justice should themselves be beyond reproof, and even in the canons dealing specifically with each of the positions named in canon, 2256, 2°, there is usually expressed in some way the requirement of a good reputation.[79]

1) The *judge* presides over the trial. The local ordinary, the *officialis,* the *vice-officiales,* and the synodal or pro-synodal judges act in this capacity.[80]

2) The *auditor,* chosen from the number of the synodal or pro-synodal judges by the ordinary, either permanently or for a specific case, has the duties of citing and examining the witnesses and of drawing up the acts of the case according to the tenor of his mandate, but he does not have the function of giving the definitive sentence.[81]

3) The *relator* or *ponens* is chosen from the college of judges by the presiding judge to report the case to the meeting of the judges and to commit the sentence to writing.[82]

4) The *promoter of justice* is appointed by the ordinary to take part in contentious cases in which the ordinary judges the public good to be endangered, and in all criminal cases.

The *defender of the bond* is appointed by the ordinary to uphold the bond of sacred ordination and of matrimony.[83]

5) A *notary* is required for each judicial process. He receives his appointment from the bishop and his assignment to a particular trial by the presiding judge.[84] He acts as secretary and as a qualified witness to whatever occurs in the course of the trial, and by

---

[79] The *officialis* and *vice-officialis* ". . . esse debent sacerdotes *integrae famae. . . .*"—canon 1573, § 4. The defender of the bond and the promoter of justice ". . . sint sacerdotes *integrae famae. . . .*"—canon 1589, § 1. The notaries and the chancellor ". . . debent esse *integrae famae. . . .*"—canon 373, § 4. The advocate and the procurator ". . . esse debent . . . *bonae famae. . . .*"—canon 1657, § 1.

[80] Canons 1572-1574.

[81] Canons 1580, § 1; 1582.

[82] Canon 1584.

[83] Canon 1586.

[84] Canons 372, § 1; 1583, § 2.

his signature makes official the documents of the process.[85] The principal notary of the diocese is the *chancellor* himself.[86]

6) The functions of the *court-messenger* or *courier* (*cursor*) and the *bailiff*, (*apparitor*) are the delivery of the citations and the announcement of the judicial acts. These functions are usually supplied in modern times through the use of registered mails.[87]

7) To the *advocate* or *attorney-at-law* are reserved those matters which pertain to the defense of a party. The duties of the *attorney-in-fact* (*procurator*) are: to represent the party, to present bills of complaint and recourses of all kinds. The advocate and attorney may be appointed by the presiding judge or by the party, but it is the judge's duty to see to it that only worthy individuals serve in these offices. Moreover, the Holy See, even since the promulgation of the Code, has seen fit to require for such positions not merely men of good reputation, as the Code itself requires in canon 1657, § 1, but men of outstanding reputation for probity of life and religious character.[88]

C. Voting in Canonical Elections

This process as it is contained in canons 160-178, is the canonical calling of a qualified person to a vacant ecclesiastical office or benefice by an assembly of lawful voters.[89] Those who are infamous by infamy of law cannot validly vote in ecclesiastical elections, just as they cannot validly perform any of the legally authorized ecclesiastical acts. Those who are infamous by infamy of fact cannot licitly vote in ecclesiastical elections, nor can they validly vote if they are deprived of that right by way of a vindicative penalty.[90]

---

[85] Canon 1585, § 1.

[86] Canons 372-374.

[87] Canons 1591-1593; 1711-1725, and especially 1719.

[88] "Procurator et advocatus esse debent Catholici . . . *honestate ac religionis fama praestantes. . . .*"—S. C. C., Instructio *Provida Mater,* 15 aug. 1936, art. 48, § 1—*AAS,* XXVIII (1936), 324; Bouscaren, *Digest,* II, 484.

[89] Parsons, *Canonical Elections,* The Catholic University of America Canon Law Studies, n. 118 (Washington, D. C.: The Catholic University of America Press, 1939), pp. 2-3.

[90] Canons 2291, 8°, 11°. Cf. canons 2366, § 2; 2368, § 1; 2336; 2389; 2342, 2°; 2331, § 2.

D. The Right of Patronage

The *ius patronatus* consists in the privileges and obligations which the Church has granted to those Catholics who founded a church, chaplaincy or benefice, or to those who have received a just title thereto from the founders.[91]

The right, an ancient institution of the Church and one of elaborate treatment in the Code, has not come into use in the United States.

Article IV. Infamy of Fact and the Giving of Testimony

One of the things which the judges must consider before admitting a witness, or when evaluating his testimony, is his reputation. One of bad reputation is under a suspicion of a certain weakness of character, which weakness may show itself by false testimony. Such false testimony may be given as the result of bribery, or simply because the individual lacks the virtues of justice and veracity.

In canon 1975 § 1, it is required that the *septimae manus* witnesses be of good reputation ("*. . . bonae famae. . . .*") In canon 1757, § 2, 1°, moreover, the *infames* are explicitly declared suspect. This certainly refers to those who are infamous by infamy of law, since upon this word there follows the phrase *"post sententiam declaratoriam vel condemnatoriam."* Blat, accordingly, stated that the word *"infames"* here refers only to infamy of law.[92]

Noval[93] and Augustine,[94] however, stated that *"infames"* here refers to both types of infamy. This seems a most reasonable assumption, and one which is not ruled out because of the inclusion of the phrase concerning the declaratory or condemnatory sentence. Canon 1757, § 2, 1°, lists with those who are infamous also those who are excommunicated and perjurers, and though excommunication and infamy of law are penalties which may be inflicted or declared by sentence, perjury and infamy of fact are not such

[91] Canon 1448.

[92] *Commentarium,* Lib. IV, p. 280.

[93] *De Iudiciis,* I, 329.

[94] *A Commentary on the New Code of Canon Law,* VII, 209.

penalties. The *sententia* may still refer to these latter terms. As for perjurers, it will pertain to the declaration of guilt and the infliction of the proper penalty according to canon 2323. For those who are infamous by infamy of fact it may be identified with the *iudicium Ordinarii* which is the official declaration of *infamia facti* according to canon 2293, § 3.[95]

Even before the declaratory or condemnatory sentence, moreover, those who are infamous by infamy of fact may be considered suspect witnesses.[96] In harmony with this view of Augustine, the phrase concerning the *sententia* may be taken to signify that, when *infamia iuris* is involved instead of *infamia facti,* those who are infamous are to be considered suspect witnesses only after sentence is passed (which means that their delicts are notorious by notoriety of law, according to canon 2197, 2°). Whenever *infamia facti* is involved, however, the individuals who are infamous may be considered suspect even in abstraction from any sentence.[97]

If the judge considers it expedient to do so, those who are infamous may be heard as suspect witnesses, that is, their testimony serves only as an indication of the truth and as adminicular proof, and furthermore they are to be heard unsworn.[98]

These provisions of the Code are in accord with the legislation and the commentaries before the Code. Historically, the two subjects of infamy and the giving of testimony in relation to each other were generally discussed by way of commentary on an important canon in the Decretals of Gregory IX.[99]

---

95 ". . . si . . . iudicium habeatur declarans aliquem infamem infamia facti, is suspectus habendus erit."—Coronata, *Institutiones,* III, 193. Cf. *supra,* pp. 65-66.

96 Augustine, VII, 209.

97 Coronata, who considers the judgment of the ordinary essential to the definition of infamy of fact (cf. *supra,* p. 65), says that even before the judgment or declaration of the ordinary the person infamous by infamy of fact should be considered suspect as a criminal, although he is not yet technically infamous.—*Institutiones,* III, 193.

98 Canon 1758.

99 C. 54, X, *de testibus et attestationibus,* II, 20. Cf. *supra,* pp. . At the time of the completion of these decretals, *infamia facti* was identified with *infamatio* or an accusation of guilt, which could be set aside by means of the canonical oath-taking (*purgatio canonica*). The canon

The canon of the Decretals, without using the term as such, specified who were the infamous persons under consideration. Those who were cleared of any guilt did not come under the restrictions of the law. But there did come under the law those who had been convicted of the crime of which they were accused, or who confessed their guilt, or who when accused were later cleared of guilt, but who were still not well thought of by others. These were barred from testifying in criminal cases. The canon of the Decretals eventually, however, became applicable to all ". . . quorum fama et existimatio apud viros prudentes et honestos graviter laesa exsistit. . . ."[100]

On the basis of the canon in the Decretals, the authors said that those who were infamous were not ordinarily to be prevented from testifying in civil cases, but they were to be prevented from testifying in criminal cases.[101] Even in certain civil cases, however, those who were infamous were to be barred from testifying: 1) in serious cases which were equal to criminal cases in import;[102] 2) in cases in which a law or precept explicitly demanded witnesses whose character was beyond all reproach;[103] 3) in matrimonial cases.[104]

---

here mentioned, however, spoke of a *gravata opinio* as existing even after the taking of the oath, and such a bad opinion, if it existed as something common among good and serious people, was infamy of fact as it gradually came to be understood. This same canon, accordingly, became a point of reference for those who wanted a good example of the law on infamy of fact and the basis for their rules regarding the giving of testimony. Cf. *supra*, pp. 26-28.

[100] Reiffenstuel, *Ius Canonicum,* Lib. II, tit. 20, n. 47.

[101] Reiffenstuel, *loc. cit.*: Farinacius, *Tractatus de Testibus* (Venetiis, 1609), q. 56, art. 2, p. 44 (hereafter cited as Farinacius); Fermosinus, VI, nn. 9-10, p. 398; Schmalzgrueber, *Ius Ecclesiasticum,* Lib. II, tit. 20, n. 16.

[102] Farinacius, q. 56, n. 107, p. 44; Fermosinus, VI, n. 15, p. 399.

[103] Farinacius, *ibid.*, n. 108.

[104] Fermosinus, *ibid.*, n. 16; Farinacius, *ibid.*, n. 109. This exclusion was in accord with the legislation of the past. The IV General Council of the Lateran (1215) had decided that, when heresay evidence was necessary in marriage cases involving consanguinity, it was permitted provided the witnesses had the necessary qualifications, in which were included ". . . that they be serious persons to whom credence could deservedly be given," and ". . . that they had learned it from persons who were not infamous

The rules which the authors before the Code accepted may even now serve to assist the judge in evaluating the testimony given by infamous individuals.

1) In any case their testimony is less credible than that of other people.[105]

2) The value of their testimony is not diminished, however, if it corroborates the testimony of another witness of such excellent character that his excellence supplies for what is objectionable in the infamous person.[106]

3) Their testimony is not of lesser value when they testify to what is probably true, or when their testimony serves as adminicular proof to what has already been surmised.[107]

4) The value of their testimony should be weighed by the judge according to the nature and the degree of their infamy.[108]

5) In any case in which the judge admits witnesses who are infamous, their testimony gives at least some indication of the truth.[109]

6) Even the slightest infamy would exclude an individual from testifying against one of noble station.[110]

7) If the witness, besides being infamous by reason of infamy of fact, reflects a character of absolute worthlessness (". . . si . . . concurrat vilitas personae. . ."), he is not to be admitted at all.[111]

---

or suspect, but from persons worthy of credence and beyond all exception, for it would be absurd to allow those to testify who repeated the words of witnesses who would themselves have been rejected."—Mansi, XXII, 1039; Martin, "Hearsay at Common Law and at Canon Law," *The Jurist,* XI (1951), 232.

[105] Farinacius, *ibid.,* n. 112.

[106] Farinacius, *ibid.,* n. 113; cf. Schmalzgrueber; ". . . testis autem infamis infamia facti . . . una cum alio teste omni exceptione maiore possit facere plenam fidem. . . ."—*Ius Ecclesiasticum,* Lib. II, tit. 20, n. 16.

[107] Farinacius, *ibid.,* n. 114.

[108] Reiffenstuel, *Ius Canonicum,* Lib. II, tit. 20, n. 47.

[109] Farinicius, *ibid.,* n. 122; Panormitanus, IV, n. 16, p. 127.

[110] Farinacius, *ibid.,* n. 116.

[111] Farinacius, *ibid.,* n. 125. This expression is the equivalent of the provision of canon 1757, § 1, 2°: "Qui ita abiectis sunt moribus ut fide digni non habeantur," who are to be considered suspect, and among whom, says Coronata, are the criminals infamous by infamy of fact.—*Institutiones,* III, 194.

The observance of these "rules" is not, of course, strictly binding upon any judge. It is impossible to set down rules which will embrace all cases of *infamia facti*. The Code, accordingly, grants great liberty to superiors, in this case ecclesiastical judges, in determining the binding force of the effects of infamy of fact in individual cases.

CONCLUSIONS

1) The Church's concept of infamy in general is an adaptation of the Roman legal system *of infamia.* The term *"infamia"* in Roman law referred to what is now known as *infamia iuris,* a vindicative penalty. The concept of *infamia facti,* an actual loss of reputation, in abstraction from any penalty, did exist in the Roman law, and was, at times, signified by the term *"turpitudo."*

2) The concept of infamy of fact has existed in the Church from its very beginning, but the term *"infamia facti"* came into common usage during the age of the medieval canonists, who identified it with *infamatio* or defamation, i.e., the accusing of another of some crime whereby the accused lost his good reputation among good and serious-minded people.

3) From the time of the medieval canonists until the Code of Canon Law the term "infamy of fact" came to be referred to a loss of reputation effected by more serious causes than mere accusations, although accusations continued to be considered causes of infamy of fact.

4) The Code of Canon Law provides us with the first legal and official descriptive definition of *infamia facti.* Whenever *infamia facti* is mentioned in the Code of Canon Law, it means, according to canon 2293, § 3: the loss of reputation which one incurs among upright Catholics because of a crime which he has committed or because of depraved morals.

5) In any doubts or disputes whether or not the details of the descriptive definition are verified in a particular case, it is left to the ordinary to decide whether or not a person is infamous by infamy of fact.

6) Though only a misdeed which fulfills the definition of a delict as furnished in canon 2197 will bring on *infamia facti,* strictly so-called, the effects of infamy of fact are sustained by all who are thought to be guilty of a delict until their innocence, e.g., because there was lacking any malice and culpability, is proved.

7) The expression "depraved morals" in the description of

infamy of fact indicates that the sins which bring on infamy of fact are public (or become publicly known), serious, and numerous or habitual.

8) Crimes and sins which bring on infamy of fact must be public, but not necessarily notorious, certainly not notorious by notoriety of law, and not even notorious by notoriety of fact, which adds to public crimes and sins the fact that they were committed in such circumstances that neither argument nor legal defense remains available to excuse them.

9) The number of those who must know of a delict or of a person's sinful life before that person can be said to be infamous by infamy of fact may be determined by the norms set down by authors for the estimation of the number of people who must know of a crime before it can be said to be public.

10) Since it pertains to the ordinary to determine whether or not infamy of fact is present in a particular case, it also belongs to the ordinary to take in hand the investigation regarding anyone who is said to have contracted infamy of fact.

11) The danger of incurring infamy of fact as described in the Code excuses one from the observance of vindicative penalties according to he provisions of canon 2290, and warrants an extraordinary absolution from censures, according to the provisions of canon 2254, and from irregularities, according to the provisions of canon 990.

12) The effects of infamy of fact are binding upon an individual only in the place where he is infamous, but infamy of fact essentially disappears only when one has, in the judgment of his ordinary, regained his good reputation in the place where he had lost it, which is to be brought about especially through a long period of amendment.

13) Public crimes, and not necessarily notorious crimes, may lead to the infamy of fact that prevents one from acting as sponsor at baptism and confirmation.

14) Only those who are notoriously infamous are to be excluded from the reception of Holy Communion. By this are meant those who have committed notorious crimes or sins, namely those which

are not merely commonly known, but which are also beyond conjecture or dispute as to their imputability.

15) Those who are notoriously infamous by reason of infamy of fact must publicly indicate repentance for their sins, and an amendment of their lives, and must publicly make satisfaction for the scandal which they have caused, before they may be permitted publicly to receive Holy Communion in the place where they are infamous.

16) Infamy of fact as an impediment to Holy Orders prevents one from being ordained, and from exercising the Orders which one already has received, only as long as the infamy, in the judgment of the ordinary, continues to exist, and only in the place where the individual is infamous.

17) Infamy of fact has no invalidating effects.

18) Infamy of fact renders witnesses suspect, and the testimony of those who are infamous by reason of infamy of fact can serve only as adminicular proof.

BIBLIOGRAPHY

Sources

Acta Apostolicae Sedis, Commentarium Officiale, Romae, 1909-1929; Civitate Vaticana, 1929—.

Acta et Decreta Sacrorum Conciliorum Recentiorum, Collectio Lacensis, 7 vols., Friburgi Brisgoviae, 1870-1892.

Bouscaren, T. Lincoln, *The Canon Law Digest,* 2 vols., and Supplement through 1948, Milwaukee, Wis.: The Bruce Publishing Co., 1934-1943-1949.

Bruns, Hermann, *Canones Apostolorum et Conciliorum Saeculorum IV-VII,* 2 vols., Berolini, 1839.

Bullarum Dilomatum et Privilegiorum Romanorum Pontificum Taurinensis Editio, 24 vols. et Appendix, Augustae Taurinorum, 1857-1872.

Codex Iuris Canonici Pii X Pontificis Maximi iussu digestus, Benedicti Papae XV auctoritate promulgatus, Praefatione, Fontium Annotatione et Indice Analytico-Alphabetico ab Emo Petro Card. Gasparri Auctus, Romae: Typis Polyglottis Vaticanis, 1917; reimpressio, 1934.

Codicis Iuris Canonici Fontes, cura Emi Petri Card. Gasparri editi, 9 vols., Romae (postea Civitate Vaticana): Typis Polyglottis Vaticanis, 1923-1939 (Vols. VII-IX, ed. cura et studio Emi Iustiniani Card. Serédi).

Collectanea S. Congregationis de Propaganda Fide, 2 vols., Romae: Typographia Polyglotta S. C. de Propaganda Fide, 1907.

Collectio Conciliorum Germaniae, 10 vols. et Index, Coloniae Augustae Agrippinensium, 1759-1790 (Vols. I-V, ed. cura J. F. Schannat-Jos. Hartzheim, 1759-1763; Vols. VI, VII, ed. cura H. Scholl, 1765-1769, Vols. IX, X, ed. cura A. Neissen, 1771-1775, Index ed. cura A. J. Hesselmann, 1790).

Concilii Plenarii Baltimorensis II, Acta et Decreta, 2. ed., Baltimorae: apud J. Murphy, 1853.

Corpus Iuris Civilis, 3 vols., Berolini: apud Weidmannos, *Codex Iustinianus,* quem recognoverit et rectractavit P. Krueger, ed. stereotypa 10, 1929; *Digesta Iustiniani Augusti,* quem recognovit Theodorus Mommsen et retractavit P. Krueger, ed. stereotypa 15, 1928; *Novellae,* quas recognovit R. Schoell, et absolvit G. Kroll, ed. stereotypa 5, 1928;

Decisiones Recensiores Rotae, 1558-1684, 19 vols. in 25, edd. P. Farinacius, P. Rubeus, et J. B. Compagnus, Venetiis, 1618-1697, Romae, 1697-1703.

Decretum Gratiani emendatum et notationibus illustratum cum glossis, Gregorii XIII, Pont. Max., iussu editum, 2 vols., Romae, 1582.

Hardouin, Jean, *Acta Conciliorum et Epistolae Decretales ac Constitutiones Summorum Pontificum,* 12 vols., Parisiis, 1714-1715.

Hinschius, Paulus, *Decretales Pseudo-Isidorianae et Capitula Angilramni,* Lipsiae, 1863.

Jaffé, Phillipus, *Regesta Pontificum Romanorum ab condita Ecclesia ad annum post Christum natum MCXCVIII,* ed. 2. correctam et auctam auspiciis Gulielmi Wattenbach curaverunt S. Lowenfeld, F. Kaltenbrunner, P. Ewald, 2 vols., Lipsiae, 1885-1888.

Kirch, Conradus, *Enchiridion Fontium Historiae Ecclesiasticae Antiquae,* 6. ed., quam curavit Leo Ueding, Barcelona: Editorial Herder, 1947.

Liber Sextus Decretalium D. Bonifatii Papae VIII, suae integritati cum Clementinis et Extravagantibus, earumque Glossis restitutus, Romae, 1582.

Mansi, Joannes, *Sacrorum Conciliorum Nova et Amplissima Collectio,* 53 vols. in 60, Parisiis, 1901-1927.

Monumenta Germaniae Historica, Legum Sectio II, *Capitularia, Capitularia Regum Francorum,* Vol. I, denuo edidit Alfredus Boretius, Hannoverae, 1883, Vol. II, Pars I, denuo ediderunt Alfredus Boretius et Victor Krause, Hannoverae, 1890.

———, Legum Sectio III, *Concilia,* Tomus I, *Concilia Aevi Merovingici,* recensuit Fridericus Maassen, Hannoverae, 1883.

———, Legum Sectio I, *Epistolae,* Tomus I et II, *Gregorii I Papae Registrum Epistolarum,* edd. Paulus Ewald et Ludovicus M. Hartmann, Berolini, 1891-1899.

Potthast, A., *Regesta Pontificum Romanorum inde ab anno post Christum Registrum Epistolarum,* edd. Paulus Ewald et Ludovicus M. Hartmann, Berolini, 1891-1899.

Potthast, A., *Regesta Pontificum Romanorum inde ab anno post Chrisitum natum 1198 ad annum 1304,* 2 vols., Berolini, 1874-1875.

Rituale Romanum, Pauli V Pontificis Maximi iussu editum, et Benedicti XIV auctum et castigatum, editio typica, 1752, Neo Eboraci: Benziger Bros., 1882.

Rituale Romanum, Pauli V. Pontificis Maximi iussu editum, aliorumque Pontificum cura recognitum, atque auctoritate Pii Papae XI ad normam Codicis Iuris accommodatum, editio typica, 1925, Neo Eboraci: Benziger Bros., 1944.

Reference Works

Abbo, John A.-Hannan, Jerome D., *The Sacred Canons,* 2 vols., St. Louis: B. Herder Book Co., 1952.

Aertnys, J.-Damen, C. A., *Theologia Moralis,* 15. ed., 2 vols., Torino: Marietti, 1947.

Aldeaseca, Fabianus ab, *De Admissione Novitiorum,* Dissertatio ad Lauream in Facultate Iuris Canonici Pontificiae Universitatis Gregorianae, Vallisoleti: Typis Sever-Cuesta, 1951.

Amos, Sheldon, *The History and the Principles of the Civil Law of Rome,* London: Kegan Paul, Trench and Co., 1883.

Andrews, E. A., *A Copious and Critical Latin-English Lexicon,* New York: Harper and Brothers, 1874.

Augustine, Charles, *A Commentary on the New Code of Canon Law,* 8 vols., St. Louis, Mo.: B. Herder Book Co., Vol. III, 5. ed., 1938, Vol. VII, 1. ed., 1921, Vol. VIII, 3. ed., 1938.

Ayrinhac, H. A., *Penal Legislation in the New Code of Canon Law,* revised by P. J. Lydon, New York: Benziger Brothers, 1936.

Azo, *Summa,* Lugduni, 1564.

Baisio, Guido a, *Commentaria in Decretorum Volumen,* Venetiis, 1577.

Bastnagel, Clement V., *The Appointment of Parochial Adjutants and Assistants,* The Catholic University of America Canon Law Studies, n. 58, Washington, D. C.: The Catholic University of America, 1930.

Beck, Henry G. J., *The Pastoral Care of Souls in South East France During the Sixth Century,* Romae: Apud Aedes Universitatis Gregorianae, 1950.

Bennington, James, *The Recipient of Confirmation,* The Catholic University of America Canon Law Studies, n. 267, Washington, D. C.: The Catholic University of America Press, 1952.

Berardi, A., *De Recidivis et Occasionariis Opusculum,* 2 vols., Faventiae: Ex Typographia Novelli, 1873.

Bernard, Fernand, *The First Year of Roman Law,* New York City: Oxford University Press, American Branch, 1906.

Berutti, Christophorus, *Institutiones Iuris Canonici,* 6 vols., Vol. VI, *De Delictis et Poenis,* Taurini-Romae: Marietti, 1938.

Beste, U., *Introductio in Codicem,* 3. ed., Collegeville, Minnesota: St. John's Abbey Press, 1946.

Blat, Albertus, *Commentarium Textus Codicis Iuris Canonici,* 6 vols., Romae: Ex Typographia Pontificia in Instituto Pii X, Lib. II, *De Personis,* 2. ed., 1921, Lib. III, Partes II-VI, *De Rebus,* 1923, Lib. V, *De Delictis et Poenis,* 1924.

Boich, Henricus, *In Quinque Decretalium Libros Commentaria,* 2 vols. in 1, Venetiis, 1576.

Borgasius, Paulus, *Tractatus de Irregularitatibus et Impedimentis Ordinum,* Venetiis, 1574.

Bouscaren, T. L.-Ellis, A., *Canon Law, A Text and Commentary,* Milwaukee: Bruce, 1946; reprint, in 1948.

Brys, J., *Iuris Canonici Compendium,* 10. ed., 2 vols., Brugis: Desclée de Brouwer, et Sii, 1947-1949.

Bucceroni, Ianuarius, *Institutiones Theologiae Moralis,* 6. ed., 4 vols., Friburgi Brisgoviae: Ex Typographia Pontificia in Instituto Pii X, 1914-1915.

Buckland, W. W., *Manual of Roman Private Law,* London: Cambridge University Press, 1925.

Cappello, F., *Tractatus Canonicus de Sacramentis,* 5 vols., Romae: Marietti, Vols. I, II, V, 5. ed., 1947, Vols. III, IV, 2. ed., 1942, 1947.

Carr, Aidan, *Vocation to the Priesthood: Its Canonical Concept,* The Catholic University of America Canon Law Studies, n. 293, Washington, D. C.: The Catholic University of America Press, 1950.

Chelodi, Joannes, *Ius Canonicum de Delictis et Poenis,* 5. ed., recognita et aucta a Pio Ciprotti, Trento: Libraria Moderna Editrice, 1943.

Christ, J. J., *Dispensation from Vindicative Penalties,* The Catholic University of America Canon Law Studies, n. 174, Washington, D. C.: The Catholic University of America Press, 1943.

Cicognani, A. G., *Canon Law,* 2. ed., Reprint, Westminster, Maryland: The Newman Press, 1949.

Claeys Bouuaert, F., et Simenon, G., *Manuale Juris Canonici,* 3 vols., Gandae et Leodii: Apud Seminarium Gandavense et Leodiense, Vol. I, 5. ed., 1939, Vol. III, 5. ed., 1943.

Cocchi, Guidus, *Commentarium in Codicem Iuris Canonici,* 8 vols., Vol. VIII, 4. ed., Taurinorum Augustae: Marietti, 1938.

Connor, Maurice, *The Administrative Removal of Pastors,* The Catholic University of America Canon Law Studies, n. 104, Washington, D. C.: The Catholic University of America, 1937.

Coronata, Matthaeus Conte a, *De Sacramentis Tractatus Canonicus,* 3 vols., Taurini-Romae: Marietti, 1943-1945.

———, *Institutiones Iuris Canonici,* 2. ed., 5 vols., Taurini-Romae: Marietti, 1939-1947.

D'Angelo, Sosius, *Ius Digestorum,* 2 vols. in 4, Vol. I, Pars I, Romae: Marietti, 1927.

De Zulueta, Francis, *The Institutes of Gaius,* 2 vols., Vol. I, Translation with notes, Oxford: Clarendon Press, 1946.

Donnellus, Hugo, *Omnia Opera Commentariorum de Iure Civili,* 12 vols., Macerata, Venetiis, 1831.

Donovan, James, *The Pastor's Obligation in Pre-Nuptial Investigation,* The Catholic University of America Canon Law Studies, n. 115, Washington, D. C.: The Catholic University of America, 1938.

Eagleton, George B., *The Diocesan Quinquennial Faculties, Formula IV,* The Catholic University of America Canon Law Studies, n. 248, Washington, D. C.: The Catholic University of America Press, 1948.

Farinacius, Prosperus, *Tractatus de Testibus,* Venetiis, 1609.

Fermosinus, N. R., *Omnia Opera, Canonica, Civilia et Criminalia,* 2. ed., 15 vols., Coloniae Allobrogum, 1741.

Ferreres, J.-Mondria, A., *Compendium Theologiae Moralis,* 17. ed., 2 vols., Barcinone: Subirana, 1949-1950.

Gasparri, Petrus, *De Sacra Ordinatione,* 2 vols., Parisiis, Lugduni, 1893.

Gass, Sylvester, *Ecclesiastical Pensions,* The Catholic University of America Canon Law Studies, n. 157, Washington, D. C.: The Catholic University of America Press, 1942.

Hannon, James, *Holy Viaticum,* The Catholic University of America Canon Law Studies, n. 314, Washington, D. C.: The Catholic University of America Press, 1951.

Haydt, John, *Reserved Benefices,* The Catholic University of America Canon Law Studies, n. 161, Washington, D. C.: The Catholic University of America Press, 1942.

Hefele, Charles, *A History of the Christian Councils,* 5 vols., Edinburgh: T. & T. Clark, Vol. I, 2. ed., 1883, Vols. II-V, 1876-1896.

Heneghan, John, *The Marriages of Unworthy Catholics: Canons 1065 and 1066,* The Catholic University of America Canon Law Studies, n. 188, Washington, D. C.: The Catholic University of America Press, 1944.

Hostiensis, Cardinalis (Henricus de Segusio), *Summa Aurea,* Lugduni, 1568.

Innocentius IV (Sinibaldo de Fieschi), *In Quinque Libros Decretalium Commentaria,* Venetiis, 1570.

Ioannes Andreae, *In Titulum de Regulis Iuris Novella Commentaria,* Venetiis, 1581.

Iorio, T., *Theologia Moralis,* 3. ed., 3 vols., Neapoli: D'Auria, 1946-1947.

Kearney, Richard, *Sponsors at Baptism According to the Code of Canon Law,* The Catholic University of America Canon Law Studies, n. 30, Washington, D. C.: The Catholic University of America, 1925.

Kurczynski, Petrus, *De Natura et Observantia Poenarum Latae Sententiae,* Katolicki Uniwersytet Lubelski Rozprawy Doktorskie, tom. 8, Lublin: Towarzystwo Naukowe Katolickiego Uniwerstytetu Lubelskiego, 1938.

Latini, Josephus, *Iuris Criminalis Philosophici Summa Lineamenta,* Taurini: Marietti, 1924.

Leage, R. W., *Roman Private Law,* 2. ed. by C. H. Ziegler, London: MacMillan and Co., 1930; reprinted, 1948.

Lee, R., *The Elements of Roman Law,* London: Sweet and Maxwell Ltd., 1944.

Lehmkuhl, Augustinus, *Theologia Moralis,* 9. ed., 2 vols., Friburgi Brisgoviae: Herder, 1898.

Liguori, St. Alphonsus Maria de, *Theologia Moralis,* 4 vols., ed. Gaudé, Romae, 1905-1912.

Lynch, George E., *Coadjutors and Auxiliaries of Bishops,* The Catholic University of America Canon Law Studies, n. 238, Washington, D. C.: The Catholic University of America Press, 1947.

Maioli, S., *De Irregularitatibus,* Romae, 1575.

Manning, Joseph L., *The Free Conferral of Offices,* The Catholic University of America Canon Law Studies, n. 219, Washington, D. C.: The Catholic University of America Press, 1945.

Maroto, Phillipus, *Institutiones Iuris Canonici,* 2 vols., Romae: Apud Commentarium pro Religiosis, Vol. I, 3. ed., 1921, Vol. II, 1919.

Maupied, Franciscus, *Juris Canonici Universi Compendium,* 2 vols., accurante J. P. Migne, Parisiis: Ex Typis L. Migne, 1861-1863.

McBride, James, *Incardination and Excardination of Seculars,* The Catholic University of America Canon Law Studies, n. 145, Washington, D. C.: The Catholic University of America Press, 1941.

McDevitt, Gerald V., *The Renunciation of an Ecclesiastical Office,* The Catholic University of America Canon Law Studies, n. 218, Washington, D. C.: The Catholic University of America Press, 1946.

Merkelbach, B., *Summa Theologiae Moralis,* 8. ed., 3 vols., Montréal: Typis Desclée de Brouwer, 1949.

Migne, J. P., *Patrologiae Cursus Completus, Series Latina,* 221 vols., Parisiis, 1844-1855.

Molina, Ludovicus de, *De Iustitia et Iure,* 3 vols. in 4, Coloniae Allobrogum, 1759.

Moretti, A., *De Sacris Functionibus,* 4 vols., Taurini: Marietti, 1936-1939.

Mortimer. R. C., *Origin of Primitive Penance in the Western Church,* Oxford: The Clarendon Press, 1939.

Naz, Raoul, *Traité de Droit Canonique,* 4 vols., Parisiis: Letouzey et Ané, 1946-1948.

Noldin, H.-Schmitt, A., *Summa Theologiae Moralis,* 3 vols., Oeniponte-Lipsiae: Sumptibus et Typis Feliciani Rauch, Vol. II, 27. ed., 1941, Vol. III, 26. ed., 1940.

Noldin, H.-Schönegger, A., *De Censuris,* 34. ed., Oeniponte-Lipsiae: Sumptibus et Typis Feliciani Rauch, 1940.

Noval, I., *Commentarium Codicis Iuris Canonici, De Processibus,* 2 vols., Taurini: Marietti, 1920-1932.

Ojetti, B., *De Romana Curia,* Romae: Ex Cooperativo Typographico Manzio, 1910.

Panormitanus, Abbas (Nicholaus de Tudeschis), *Commentaria in Quinque Libros Decretalium,* 5 vols. in 8, Venetiis, 1588.

Parsons, Anscar J., *Canonical Elections,* The Catholic University of America Canon Law Studies, n. 118, Washington, D. C.: The Catholic University of America, 1936.

Phillips, George, *Du Droit Ecclésiastique dans ses Principes Généraux,* 2. ed., traduit, revuée et corrigée par J-P. Crouzet, 3 vols., Paris: Jacques Lecoffre et Cie, Libraires, 1855.

———, *Compendium Iuris Ecclesiastici,* 3. ed. (1. ed. Latinae versionis), Ratisbonae: Sumptibus et Typis Georgii Josephi Manz, 1875.

Pignatelli, I., *Consultationes Canonicae,* 11 vols. in 5, Coloniae Allobrogum, 1700.

Piscetta, A.-Gennaro, A., *Elementa Theologiae Moralis,* 5. ed., 7 vols., Torino: Società Editrice Internazionale, 1941-1943.

Popek, Alphonse, *The Rights and Obligations of Metropolitans,* The Catholic University of America Canon Law Studies, n. 260, Washington, D. C.: The Catholic University of America Press, 1947.

Prince, John E., *The Diocesan Chancellor,* The Catholic University of America Canon Law Studies, n. 167, Washington, D. C.: The Catholic University of America, 1942.

Prümmer, Dominicus M., *Manuale Theologiae Moralis,* 3. ed., 3 vols., Friburgi Brisgoviae: Herder & Co., 1923.

———, *Manuale Iuris Canonici in Usum Scholarum,* 5. ed., Friburgi Brisgoviae: Herder & Co., 1927.

Quinn, Joseph, *Documents Required for the Reception of Orders,* The Catholic University of America Canon Law Studies, n. 266, Washington, D. C.: The Catholic University of America Press, 1948.

Raymond of Peñafort, *Summa Iuris,* ed. Msgr. J. Serra, Barcelona: Sobs. de López Robert y Cª. impressores, 1945.

Regatillo, E., *Institutiones Iuris Canonici,* 4. ed., 2 vols., Sal Terrae: Santander, 1951.

———, *Ius Sacramentarium,* 2 vols., Sal Terrae: Santander, 1945-1946.

Reiffenstuel, A., *Ius Canonicum Universum,* 5 vols. in 7, Parisiis, 1864-1870.

Rufinus, *Die Summa Decretorum,* ed. H. Singer, Paderborn: Druck und Verlag von Ferdinand Schöningh, 1902.

Salucci, Raffaele, *Il Diritto Penale secondo il Codice Diritto Canonico,* 2 vols., Subiaco: Tipografia dei Monasteri, 1926-1930.

Santamaria, Peña F., *Comentarios ad Código Canónico,* 6 vols., Madrid, 1919-1922.

Schaefer, Timotheus, *De Religiosis ad Normam Codicis Iuris Canonici,* 3. ed., Romae: Typis Polyglottis Vaticanis, 1940.

Schmalzgrueber, Franciscus, *Ius Ecclesiasticum Universum,* 5 vols. in 12, Romae, 1843-1845.

Shuhler, Ralph, *Privileges of Regulars to Absolve and Dispense,* The Catholic University of America Canon Law Studies, n. 186, Washington, D. C.: The Catholic University of America Press, 1943.

Simpson, S.-Stone, J., *Cases and Readings on Law and Society in Three Books,* Book I, *Law and Society in Evolution,* American Casebook Series, St. Paul, Minn.: West Publishing Co., 1948.

Sipos, Stephanus, *Enchiridion Iuris Canonici,* Pécs: Typographia "Haladás R. T.," 1926.

Slavkosky, Andrew, *The Canonical Episcopal Visitation of the Diocese,* The Catholic University of America Canon Law Studies, n. 142, Washington, D. C.: The Catholic University of America Press, 1941.

Sohm, Rudolph, *The Institutes,* 3. ed., Oxford: At the Clarendon Press, 1926.

Sole, Jacobus, *Praelectiones in Lib. V Codicis Iuris Canonici, De Delictis et Poenis,* Romae: Pustet, 1920.

Stadler, Joseph, *Frequent Holy Communion,* The Catholic University of America Canon Law Studies, n. 263, Washington, D. C.: The Catholic University of America Press, 1947.

Suárez, Emmanuel, *De Remotione Parochorum*, Romae: Scuola Tipografica Pio X, 1931.

Suarez, Franciscus, *Omnia Opera*, Vivès editio, ed. Carolus Berton, 26 vols., Parisiis, 1856-1861, Vol. XXIII, *De Censuris*, 1861.

Sylvester (Prieras), *Summa Silvestrina*, 2 vols., Venetiis, 1601.

Thomas Aquinas, St., *Summa Theologica*, 5 vols., Taurini: Marietti, 1938.

Van Hove, A., *Tractatus de Sanctissima Eucharistia*, 2. ed., Mechlinae: H. Dessain, 1941.

Vermeersch, A.-Creusen, J., *Epitome Iuris Canonici*, 3 vols., Bruxellis: Dessain, Vol. I, 6. ed., 1937, Vol. II, 5. ed., 1934, Vol. III, 5. ed., 1936.

Vogelpohl, Henry, *The Simple Impediments to Holy Orders*, The Catholic University of America Canon Law Studies, n. 224, Washington, D. C.: The Catholic University of America Press, 1945.

Waldron, Joseph F., *The Minister of Baptism*, The Catholic University of America Canon Law Studies, n. 170, Washington, D. C.: The Catholic University of America Press, 1942.

Weller, Phillip, *The Roman Ritual*, 3 vols., Vol. I, *The Sacraments and Processions*, Milwaukee: Bruce, 1950.

Wernz, F.-Vidal, P., *Ius Canonicum ad Codicis Normam Exactum*, 7 vols. in 8, Romae: Apud Aedes Universitatis Gregorianae, Vol. II, 3. ed., 1943, Vol. IV, Pars I, 1934, Vol. VI, 1927-1928.

Woywod, Stanislaus, *A Practical Commentary on the Code of Canon Law*, 4. ed., 2 vols., New York: Wagner, 1929.

Articles

Anonymous, "Entscheidung der Konzilskongregation, betr. die Zulassung öffernt-licher Sünder zur hl. Kommunion," *Archiv für katholisches Kirchenrecht*, CIII (1923), 162.

Anonymous, "Circa l'ammisione di pubblici concubinari alla S. Communione," *Il Monitore Ecclesiastico*, XXXV (1923), 237.

Anonymous, "Intorno alla irregolarità che si contrae colla infamia," *Il Monitore Ecclesiastico*, X, Parte II (1898), 10-17.

Hilling, N., "Kirchliches Officium und Potestas Ordinaria"—*Archiv für katholisches Kirchenrecht*, CXVII (1937), 433-435.

Martin, Thomas O., "Hearsay at Common Law and at Canon Law"—*The Jurist*, XI (1951), pp. 58-76 and 226-250.

Oesterle, G., "Casus ad Canonem 855 C. J. C."—*Perfice Munus*, XIV (1939), 739-753.

Periodicals

Archiv für katholisches Kirchenrecht, Innsbruck, 1857-1861; Mainz, 1862—

Jurist, The, Washington, D. C., 1941—

Monitore Ecclesiastico, Il, Romae, 1876—

Perfice Munus, Torino, 1926—

Abbreviations

AAS—*Acta Apostolicae Sedis.*
Abbo-Hannon—*The Sacred Canons.*
Augustine—*A Commentary on the New Code of Canon Law.*
Beck—*The Pastoral Care of Souls in South East France During the Sixth Century.*
Bernard-Sherman—*The First Year of Roman Law.*
Beste—*Introductio in Codicem.*
Blat—*Commentarium Textus Codicis Iuris Canonici.*
Boich—*Commentaria in Quinque Libros Decretalium.*
Borgasius—*Tractatus de Irregularitibus et Impedimentis Ordinum.*
Bouscaren-Ellis—*Canon Law, A Text and Commentary.*
Bruns—*Canones Apostolorum et Conciliorum Saeculorum IV-VII.*
Bucceroni—*Institutiones Theologiae Moralis.*
Buckland—*Manual of Roman Private Law.*
Christ—*Dispensation from Vindicative Penalties.*
Cicognani—*Canon Law.*
Claeys Bouuaert-Simenson—*Manuale Juris Canonici.*
Commentaria—Panormitanus, *Commentaria in Quinque Libros Decretalium.*
D'Angelo—*Ius Digestorum.*
Decisiones Recensiores—*Decisiones Recensiores Rotae, 1558-1684.*
Digest—*The Canon Law Digest.*
Eagleton—*The Diocesan Quinquennial Faculties, Formula IV.*
Farinacius—*Tractatus de Testibus.*
Fermosinus—*Omnia Opera, Canonica, Civilis et Criminalia.*
Ferreres-Mondria—*Compendium Theologiae Moralis.*
Fontes—*Codicis Iuris Canonici Fontes.*
Genicot-Salsmans—*Institutiones Theologiae Moralis.*
Hardouin—*Acta Conciliorum et Epistolae Decretales ac Constitutiones Summorum Pontificum.*
Haydt—*Reserved Benefices.*
Hefele—*A History of the Christian Councils.*
Hinschius—*Decretales Pseudo-Isidorianae et Capitula Angilramni.*
Kirch—*Enchiridion Fontium Historiae Ecclesiasticae Antiquae.*
Kurczynski—*De Natura et Observantia Poenarum Latae Sententiae.*
Leage—*Roman Private Law.*
Lehmkuhl—*Theologia Moralis.*
Lynch—*Coadjutors and Auxiliaries of Bishops.*
Maioli—*De Irregularitatibus.*
Mansi—*Sacrorum Conciliorum Nova et Amplissima Collectio.*
Maroto—*Institutiones Iuris Canonici.*
McBride—*Incardination and Excardination of Seculars.*
McDevitt—*The Renunciation of an Ecclesiastical Office.*
Merkelbach—*Summa Theologiae Moralis.*
MGH—*Monumenta Germaniae Historica.*

PL—Migne, *Patrologia Latina.*
Naz—*Traité de Droit Canonique.*
Noldin-Schmitt—*Summa Theologiae Moralis.*
Piscetta-Gennaro—*Elementa Theologiae Moralis.*
Popek—*The Rights and Obligations of Metropolitans.*
Sohm—*The Institutes.*
Stadler—*Frequent Holy Communion.*
Vogelpohl—*The Simple Impediments to Holy Orders.*
Waldron—*The Minister of Baptism.*
Weller—*The Roman Ritual.*
Wernz-Vidal—*Ius Canonicum ad Codicis Normam Exactum.*

ALPHABETICAL INDEX

BIOGRAPHICAL NOTE

FRANK J. RODIMER was born on October 25, 1927, in Rockaway, New Jersey. He reecived his elementary and the first year of his high school education in the Rockaway Public Schools. In 1941 he entered Seton Hall Preparatory School, South Orange, New Jersey, from which he was graduated in June, 1944. In that same year he entered St. Charles College, Catonsville, Maryland, and in 1946 began the philosophical course at St. Mary's Seminary, Paca Street, Baltimore, Maryland. He received the degree of Bachelor of Arts from this seminary in June, 1947. In September, 1947, he began the course in Theology at Immaculate Conception Seminary, Darlington, New Jersey, and in 1950 entered Theological College, at The Catholic University of America, Washington, D. C. He received the degree of Licentiate in Sacred Theology from The Catholic University in 1951. He was ordained to the priesthood on May 19, 1951, in the Cathedral of Saint John the Baptist, Paterson, New Jersey. In October, 1951, he enrolled in the School of Canon Law of The Catholic University of America. He received the degree of Baccalaureate in Canon Law in June, 1952, and the degree of Licentiate in Canon Law in June, 1953.

CANON LAW STUDIES*

349. BOTTOMS, REV. ARCHIBALD M., J.C.L., The discretionary authority of the ecclesiastical judge in matrimonial trials of the first instance.
350. KEKUMANO, REV. CHARLES A., A.B., J.C.L., The secret archives of the diocesan curia.
351. MCGRATH, REV. ROBERT EAMON, O.M.I., J.C.L., The local superior in non-exempt clerical congregations.
352. MCMANUS, REV. FREDERICK RICHARD, A.B., J.C.L., The Congregation of Sacred Rites.
353. RODIMER, REV. FRANK J., A.B., S.T.L., J.C.L., The canonical effects of infamy of fact.
354. ROUILLARD, REV. JACQUES, A.B., Ph.B., J.C.L., Une étude comparé du droit canonique et du droit civil paroissal de la Province de Québec dans l'administration des biens paroissaux.
355. RYAN, REV. THOMAS C., J.C.L., The juridical effects of the *sanatio in radice*.
356. SULLIVAN, REV. BERNARD OWENS, J.C.L., Legislation and requirements for permissible cohabitation in invalid marriages.
357. TATARCZUK, REV. VINCENT ANTHONY, A.B., S.T.L., J.C.L., Infamy of law.

* For a complete list of the available numbers of this series apply to the Catholic University of America Press, 620 Michigan Ave, N.E., Washington 17, D. C., for a general catalogue.

www.ingramcontent.com/pod-product-compliance
Lightning Source LLC
LaVergne TN
LVHW050226080826
844660LV00012B/483

* 9 7 8 0 8 1 3 2 2 5 2 1 0 *